KNOWLEDGE, DISSEMINATION AND PUBLICATION

About the Authors

Partha Pratim Ray, M.A., M. Lib. I. Sc., M. Phil, Ph.D. in Library and Information Science is a working librarian and guest faculty of Institute of Education, Visva-Bharati. Dr. Ray has contributed more than thirty-five research papers in journals of national and international repute and chapters to eight books. Besides Tagore's literature his area of specialization includes role of information communication in society and bibliometric study. Dr. Ray is the author of the book entitled: *Tagore in Print: A Comparative Study Before and After Expiry of Copyright* (2012).

Bimal Kanti Sen (1938) M. Lib. I. Sc. Ph.D in Library and Information Scinece served INSDOC for more than 30 years in various capacities. He served the University of Malaya as a Visiting Professor from 1995 to 1999. Dr. Sen has guided more than 50 students for their dissertations and contributed more than 200 papers, authored/edited one dozen books, wrote about 30 course materials of Indira Gandhi National Open University, and edited half a dozen journals including among others *Annals of Library and Information Science; Malaysian Journal of Library Bulletin.* **His books among others include *On Bengali Scientific Terminology* (Bengali); *Glossary of Library and Information Science Terms* (English-Bengali), *In Search of Knowledge; Directory of Scientific Research Institutions in India*, 2nd ed.; *Growth of Scientific Periodicals in India* (1788-1900); *Growth of Scientific Periodicals in India* (1901-1947) *DDC Readymade;* and *Chemical Terminology* (English – Bengali).**

Knowledge, Dissemination and Publication

Tagore in the Perspective of Information Science

Partha Pratim Ray
and
B.K. Sen

CONCEPT PUBLISHING COMPANY PVT., LTD.
NEW DELHI-110059

ISBN-13 : 978-93-5125-050-0

First Published 2014

Published and Printed by

Concept
Since 1974

Concept Publishing Company Pvt. Ltd.
A/15-16, Commercial Block, Mohan Garden
New Delhi-110059 (India)
T: 25351460, 25351794, *F*: 091-11-25357109
E: publishing@conceptpub.com, W: www.conceptpub.com
Editorial Office: H-13, Bali Nagar, New Delhi-110 015, India.

Cataloging in Publication Data—*Courtesy:* D.K. Agencies (P) Ltd. <docinfo@dkagencies.com>

Ray, Partha Pratim.
Knowledge, dissemination and publication : Tagore in the perspective of information science / Partha Pratim Ray and B.K. Sen.
p. cm.
Includes bibliographical references and index.
ISBN 9789351250500

1. Tagore, Rabindranath, 1861-1941—Criticism and interpretation. 2. Tagore, Rabindranath, 1861-1941—Knowledge—Education. I. Sen, B. K., joint author. II. Title.

DDC 370.1 23

Dedicated
to
Our Mother
who
Taught us
Basic Lessons of Life

Preface

Rabindranath Tagore (1861-1941) essentially known to the world as a poet, but his literary creations include drama, short stories, songs, essays, novels, letters which have been published in thirty-one bulky volumes of his '*collected works*'. The journey of creation starts with the publication of verse *Kavi-Kahini* in 1878 and ends with the publication of *Arogya* (Verse), *Janmadine* (Verse), *Galpasalpa* (Stories and poems), *Sabhyatar Samkat* (Address), *Asramer Rup O Vikas* (Essays) in 1941, the year of poet's departure from this world. Tagore took painting late in life at the age of sixty-seven, yet achieved distinction as a painter by painting more than two thousand drawings and paintings. He was an editor, dramatist, social, political, religious, aesthetic thinker, educational innovator, pioneer of rural reconstruction programme in India. Rabindranath was more than a literary icon, a cultural ambassador, a believer of one *One World* concept, a myriad-minded poet and writer ('*poeta et scriptor myrianous*'), a universal man.

Rabindranath was not an ideal dreamer. He tried to give his ideas on society, religion, education, rural reconstruction to a concrete shape with the establishment of his experimental *asram-school* at *Santiniketan* (Abode of Peace) in 1901 and rural reconstruction centre at *Sriniketan* (Abode of Lakshmi) in 1921. Tagore's educational philosophy is based on fullness and conversion of individual fullness to social fullness. Tagore's vision of education has been reflected in different essays like *Sikshar Herpher* (Our Education and its Incongruities), *Siksha-Samskar* (Reforms in Education), *Siksha-Samasya* (The Problem of Education), *Dharmasiksha* (Religious Education), *Laksya O Siksha* (Aims and

Education), *Strisiksha* (The Education of Women), *Sikshar Bahan* (The Vehicle of Education), *My School*. Tagore's idea of knowledge is based on his educational philosophy. He wished to disseminate knowledge to the masses through different indigenous functions and festivals and also library system. Based on Tagore's vision of knowledge and dissemination, publication for social development the present work is divided into three segments:

Knowledge and Dissemination

Rabindranath believed that "whatever is worth knowing is knowledge. It should be known equally by men and women—not for the sake of practical utility, but for the sake of knowing...The desire to know is the law of the nature". As "light unites, darkness separates, knowledge is the greatest factor in the unification of mankind". Knowledge helps to generate "power of thinking and power of imagination", which "are undoubtedly two very essential faculties for adult life". It has to be shared and disseminated. It can be achieved through living and loving human contact since "the fundamental purpose of education is not merely to enrich ourselves through the fullness of knowledge, but also to establish the bond of love and friendship between man and man". The first paper in this segment 'Tagore's Vision of Knowledge and its Dissemination' attempts to understand Tagore's concept of knowledge and methods he adopted to disseminate it for social benefit.

Rabindranath gathered first experience of rural life at the age of 19 in their family state in Silaidaha and Patisar. As he understand "...the sorrow and poverty of the villages became clear to me, and I began to grow restless to do something about it... from that time forward I continually endeavoured to find out how villagers mind could be aroused, so that they themselves could accept responsibility for their own lives". The idea takes concrete shape with the establishment of rural reconstruction programme at Sriniketan in November 1921 aiming to make villagers self-reliant and self-respecting, and competent to make efficient use of resources for the fullest development of their physical, social, economic and intellectual potential and abilities; and to get them acquainted with the cultural tradition of their own. For this purpose Tagore laid full emphasis on collection and dissemination of information. The underlying principle of the project was to "... liberate these few villages in every respect so that all may receive education, a breeze of joy may blow once again, songs and music, recitation from epics and scriptures may fill them, as of yore". The second paper entitled "Knowledge Dissemination in Tagore's Model of Rural Reconstruction: An Overview" attempts to highlight how information on rural Bengal was collected, disseminated and utilized for preparing rural development plan and its implementation. It also tries to highlight the functions of the Rural Reconstruction Centre for dissemination of information to rural masses.

Tagore believed that "for the fundamental purpose of education it is not merely to enrich ourselves through the fullness of knowledge, but also to establish the bond of love and friendship between man and man". For that he suggests "the higher educational institutions should assimilate knowledge from all sources and disseminate it for benefit of the masses in order to strengthen their own foundation". Keeping this in mind ever since Rabindranath Tagore conceived the idea of Visva-Bharati, development of library for collection, preservation and dissemination of knowledge were an integral part of his institution. His concern in this regard is amply reflected in many of his speeches and writings wherein his concern for both philosophical as well as functional aspects of library service finds a poignant place. As a man of action Rabindranath tried to give his vision of library a concrete shape in Visva-Bharati. The paper 'Tagore's Vision of Library: A Study' aims to recapture the vision of one of the most sensitive minds in the field of library service by applying principles of literature search and bibliometrics.

Tagore gave stress on rural library services as he felt "a natural bond between education in the schools and colleges and the country outside them is immensely necessary". This is necessary to fulfill the objectives of education as "the highest education is that which does not give us information but makes our life in harmony with all existence". He wanted to create cultured knowledge environment and also communicate necessary knowledge and skill for rendering service to the villagers. For this along with other development programmes Tagore started rural library services through the establishment of mobile library 'Chalantika'. The 'Role of Public Library in Tagore's Model of Rural Reconstruction: A Study' aims to study Tagore's experiment with public library service as an integral part of rural reconstruction programme at Sriniketan.

Bibliometric Study of Select Writings of Tagore

Rabindranath Tagore has composed more than two thousand songs. His songs known as Rabindra Sangit have become a symbol of cultural ethos of both India and Bangladesh. The paper 'Songs of Rabindranath Tagore: A Bibliometric Study' attempts to study the growth of Rabindra Sangit, Tagore's writings on songs in different literary forms throughout the different phases of his literary career, as well as its publication trends with the help of bibliometric technique.

Published letters written by Rabindranath Tagore counts to four thousand ninety-eight. Besides family members and Santiniketan associates Tagore wrote to different personalities like litterateurs, poets, artists, editors, thinkers, scientists, politician, statesman, government officials. These letters form a substantial part of intellectual output of 'Tagoreana'. The paper entitled 'Letters of Rabindranath Tagore: A Bibliometric Study" attempts to study the growth pattern of letters written by Rabindranath and to find out whether it follows Bradford's law. Rabindranath wrote letters throughout his literary career to three hundred fifteen persons covering all aspects such as literary, social, educational, philosophical as well as personal matters and it does not strictly satisfy Bradford's bibliometric law.

Rabindranath received Nobel Prize for Gitanjali (Songs Offerings) in 1913 which is a collection of poems from different Kavyagrantha (book of poems). The paper entitled 'Gitanjali: A Bibliometric Study' attempts has been made to study the growth of poems of Gitanjali, their lengths, places and dates of writings, use of words, rank frequency of different words and to find out whether Gitanjali follows any bibliometric law. The study also tries to find justification of the title Gitanjali with the help of Zipf's law. Attempts have also been made to find out whether rank-frequency distributions of word in Gitanjali follow Zipf's law.

Tagore in Print: An Assessment of Quality of Publications

Rabindranath gave copyright of his intellectual output to Visva-Bharati. In a letter dated 18th September 1922 he wrote, "I have given the right of all my Bengali books to Visva-Bharati in a deed and relieved now". Accordingly Visva-Bharati enjoyed copyright of Rabindranath as per the then existing law up to December 1991. Later, the Indian Parliament enhanced the copyright period keeping in mind the Tagore's work and Visva-Bharati, from 50 years to 60 years after the expiry of the author. The extended period of copyright of Rabindranath ended in December 2001. Now private publishers are free to publish writings of Rabindranath. The paper 'Tagoreana in Copyright-Free Phase: An assessment of Quality of Publications' tries to find out whether complete, accurate Rabindranath's Bengali writings are being published by private publishers at an affordable cost. At the same time the article tries to address the questions like: What kind of publications should be treated as standard? Whether Tagoreana is being published simultaneously by large private publishing houses as well as small and new publishers in Bengali? What percentage of Tagoreana is being published by private publishers?

Rabindranath received Nobel Prize for *Gitanjali* (Song Offerings) in 1913 which is a collection of poems from different *Kavyagrantha* (book of poems). India Society of London first published English version of *Gitanjali* on 1st November 1912. The next edition of *Gitanjali* was published in the next year (March 1913) by Macmillan and Company, London. Visva-Bharati publishing unit known as Visva-Bharati Granthan Vibhaga (VBGV) established in 1923 to publish Tagore's writings. After expiry of copyright Private publishers are publishing *Gitanjali* like other writings of Tagore. The article entitled '100 Years of Publication of Gitanjali: A Study' attempts to assess the quality of publication of *Gitanjali* published by private publishers before establish of VBGV and after expiry of copyright.

Santiniketan
Vasanta Utsava' 2013

Dr. Partha Pratim Ray
and
Prof. B.K. Sen

Acknowledgements

We owe a deep sense of gratitude to several persons—academicians, colleagues and institutions for accomplishment of the present work. It is difficult to express our gratitude to all of them by name. Yet, firstly we express our deepest gratitude to late Dr. Bidhan Chandra Biswas, Associate Professor, Department of Library and Information Science, University of Kalyani for his continuous encouragement, keen interest and valuable suggestions.

It is a pleasure to acknowledge gratitude to the staff members of the Central Library, Institute of Education Library and Sangit Bhavana Library of Visva-Bharati for their co-operation in extensive use of the library resources.

It is our privilege to express gratitude to the Curator and the staff-members of the Archives, Library as well as Audio-Visual section, Tagorean Research Centre Rabindra-Bhavana, Visva-Bharati, for their kind co-operation and help.

Last but not the least, we would like to express our sincere indebtedness to our family members for their loving support and sacrifice of leisure.

Partha Pratim Ray
B.K. Sen

Contents

SECTION-I

Knowledge and Dissemination

One

Tagore's Vision of Knowledge and its Dissemination

Introduction

Tagore founded his ashram school at Santiniketan in 1901 when Indian renaissance of the 20th century, inspired by Raja Rammohun Roy had reached its peak. At that time there was a strong demand in the country for reorienting Indian education system on true nationalistic pattern. Tagore was associated with this movement. But later on Tagore withdrew himself from national agitation of Bengal and converted his institution into a centre of Indian culture as "a new restlessness of spirit" overtook him. He invited people from different parts of India as teachers and pupils to work together with a view to realizing the fundamental unity underlying the different cultural traditions of the country. As a result Visva Bharati was founded on 23 December 1918. According to poet "…in my institution I tried to make provisions for three aspects of freedom—freedom of mind, freedom of heart and freedom of will. I have deep-rooted conviction that through freedom man attains his fullness of growth"[1]. But Tagore's concept of education for knowledge generation, communication and utilization was not detached from the society. Education has to play a distinct role for social development. To achieve this social responsibility of education, Tagore adopted policies for community education programme for rural development associating his institution with rural Bengal's economic, social and cultural outlook.

Concept of Knowledge

According to Tagore "whatever is worth knowing, is knowledge. It should be known equally by men and women—not for the sake of practical utility, but for the sake of knowing…The desire to know is the law of the nature"[2]. He further clarifies "We have come to this world, to accept it or nor merely to know it. We may become powerful by knowledge, but attain fullness by sympathy. The highest education is that which does not merely give us information but makes our life harmony with all existence"[3]. As "light unites, darkness separates, knowledge is the greatest factor in the unification of mankind"[4]. Knowledge helps to generate "power of thinking and power of imagination", which "are undoubtedly two very essential faculties for adult life"[5]. Tagore also stressed, "a dry, factual knowledge of the past is not enough; such knowledge must be vivid and real[6] because "knowledge is the thing of spirit, and we can never think of its being measured in terms of bricks and mortars"[7]. Knowledge includes all training that is useful for service to the mankind. Tagore clearly stated "knowledge has two departments: one, pure knowledge; and other, utilitarian knowledge"[8]. For developing utilitarian knowledge instead of bookish knowledge, a cultural environment conducive for knowledge generation should be developed. Recognising this aspect Tagore established in the *Santiniketan Asrama* a field for the pursuit of culture on a wide scale. For proper nourishment of India culture Santiniketan School laid emphasis not only on cultivation of knowledge within narrow limits defined by textbooks prescribed in schools but also on all kinds of arts and crafts, dance, music and play as well as knowledge and skill necessary for rendering service to the village. He further suggests "the foundation of knowledge becomes sound and effective if the acquisition of it approaches from known to unknown…We can achieve the power to accept and realize the objects of knowledge which are indirect and unfamiliar only when we have fully and truly mastered the objects of knowledge which are known and familiar"[9].

Tagore does not appreciate any knowledge which is metaphysical intuition, but he has enough sympathy and regards for discursive knowledge which prevents love from degenerating into spineless and drab sentimentality. For this ultimate object of knowledge-dissemination is to build up "the man per excellence".

Knowledge Dissemination

The universe of knowledge is the product of collective endeavour of all men of all the times all over the countries, every man has birthright to inherit it and it is his duty to contribute and disseminate. Thus acquisition of knowledge is not enough. It is to be communicated and shared to achieve social goals. It can be achieved through living and loving human contact since "the fundamental purpose of education is not merely to enrich ourselves through the fullness of knowledge, but also to establish the bond of love and friendship between man and man"[10]. This is because "the aspiration of a man for an ever expanding fullness has two aspects that are interrelated: one is individual fullness, and the other is social fullness; there is no gap between the two"[11]. To achieve total fullness the expanding knowledge and growing power at the disposal of modern society must be combined together with strengthening and deepening of the sense of social responsibility and a keener appreciation of moral and spiritual values.

For generation as well as dissemination of knowledge, educational institutions have a great role to play. Tagore suggests "the higher educational institutions should assimilate knowledge from all sources and disseminate it for the benefit of the masses in order to strengthen their own foundation"[12]. To foster proper communication of knowledge Tagore laid emphasis on mind-to-mind communication in mother tongue. As he narrates "my mind is not separate from yours. Had it been so, no communication between mind and mind is possible"[13]. Knowledge acquired from foreign sources is not properly assimilated, it is like artificial limb grafted from outside through surgical process. "The most important aid to that process of assimilation", Tagore observed, "is the mother tongue. All educational food is digested and assimilated through the chemical action of that language". "The mother tongue", he added "acts like mother milk"[14]. The necessity of knowledge dissemination has clearly been stated in one of the objectives of *Sriniketan* (Institute of Rural Reconstruction) "to carry the knowledge and experience gained in the class-room and farm to the villages"[15].

Educational Institution

Tagore's educational philosophy is based on "unity of mind". It is an all round drawing out of the best in child and man-body, mind and spirit. According to him, "education is not merely imparting of information; man has not been born to carry a load of information; the purpose at the root of life has to be realized. The aim of education is to realize fully through knowledge and action the entire purpose of human life"[16]. To attain this objective, Tagore asked for our own original contribution to the stock of world's knowledge. The test of a successful educational system of a country, according to him, depends on realization of the importance of knowledge and assimilation of the essential culture and scholarship of one's own country. The central idea of Tagore's educational philosophy can be clearly observed from the meaning of Visva-Bharati itself which is derived from Sanskrit concept '*Yatra visvam bhavatyekanidam*' where the world makes its nest in a single home or '*Yatra Bharati Visvam Ekam Bhavati*' where the world becomes one in India. Thus, Visva-Bharati represents India where she has her wealth of mind which is for all. Visva-Bharati acknowledges India's obligation to offer to others the hospitality of her best culture and India's right to accept from others their best.

Educational institutions should derive knowledge as far as possible, directly from nature and life. The process of acquiring knowledge independently from direct sources is a good exercise for our intellectual powers like observation, experimentation, and reasoning in an easy, natural and pleasurable way. As "knowledge associated with joy and satisfaction increases our power of learning;

consequently our power of reception, appreciation, thinking and judgment develops easily and naturally"[17]. For this reason the curriculum proposed by Tagore was a form of activity curriculum in which students are required to master not only some knowledge and information but also some skill and attitude, through their active participation in productive and creative activities. The teacher as a living source of knowledge has a great role to play in this respect. Tagore welcomed persons with superior personalities and missionary spirit as teachers, as he felt that the teacher should have the qualities to become friends as well as guide to the pupils in discovering the sources of knowledge and understanding, joy and creation to help the students in attaining the fullness of growth in body, mind and spirit.

Tagore invited learned personalities in Visva-Bharati and requested them to write easy-to-understand textbooks on different disciplines. As a result two series of textbooks were published titled *Visva-Vidya Samgraha* (collection of universal knowledge) and *Loka Siksha Granthamala* (series of books for mass education). To disseminate knowledge for the masses *Loka-Siksha Samsad* was formed at Sriniketan in 1936. The mass education became a reality through sustained effort of some celebrated scholars by virtue of their whole-hearted efforts to bring knowledge and education within the reach of millions of readers and learners in remote villages through the medium of mother tongue Bengali.

Library

For the preservation, nurturing and development of knowledge a library is but *sine qua non*. For thousands of years learned celebrities established libraries in various parts of the world whereby knowledge generated have been preserved for the use of the prosperity. Hence, it is no wonder that the idea of setting up a library was conceived by Maharshi Devendranath, father of Rabindranath simultaneously with the idea of establishing Santiniketan *Asrama*. In 1888 Maharshi Devendranath Tagore made a trust deed providing an annual grant for maintenance of Santiniketan House and adjoining grounds, and dedicated the *Asrama* to all seekers of truth without discrimination to caste, creed etc, who were free to come and stay to meditate on the *Supreme Being*. No injury to animal life was to be committed and no worship of idols to be revealed. On the objectives of the development of education the deed indicates," in pursuance of the need of enhancement of the quality of living in the *Asrama* the trustees were empowered to establish a *Brahmavidyalaya* at Santiniketan and a library"[18]. Immediately after the establishment of *Asrama* on 19th October 1888 a small library came up and started functioning in a room of Santiniketan House. Tagore wrote," The collection of our revered father's book was kept in one of the three rooms. We first look after the proper preservation of books and manuscripts. What occupied our thought thereafter was where we could fix students"[19].

Before the establishment of *Brahmacharya Asrama* at Santiniketan by Rabindranath Tagore on 22 December, 1901 the *Asrama* library got enriched with his big personal collection Tagore's biographer Prabhat Kumar Mukhopadhyaya (1892-1985) took charge of the *Asrama* library in the month of July 1910 following which the library started developing in a scientific way. Tagore presented most of the books then added to the library. Rabindranath purchased as well as received books on various subjects. After going through them he presented them to the library. Even today one can find many books in the stack of Visva-Bharati library with marginal notes by Rabindranath. The total collection of the library in the year 1911-12 was nearly four thousand.

In December 1921 Visva-Bharati was declared as a National University with international outlook. Thereafter, the library started growing rapidly through regular purchase as well as gifts from various countries and personalities. The Annual Report of Visva-Bharati 1921-22 records, "the library at Santiniketan is one of the special features of Visva Bharati. The library possesses a very good collection of books on Sanskrit, Pali and Prakrit, a valuable collection of Chinese and Tibetan Books. The Indian vernaculars are well represented specially Bengali, Hindi and Gujarati. It also contains a very unique collection of books on Indology and Art, chiefly in French and German. We are indebted for this collection to our friends overseas who had made a free gift of the books in this section. The total number of books is about 16000 at present. The library received about one hundred magazines and periodicals and oriental journals as presentation. The work of classification and cataloguing in accordance with standard decimal system is proceeding. Extensive additions have been made to the library building and stack room has been fitted with iron shelves. Satisfactory arrangements have been made for the proper care and keep of our valuable collection"[20].

Visva-Bharati library regularly received books as gifts from scholars all over the globe. In the year 1925 the library received 500 books as gifts from Italy during the period of Mussolini in Italian language (accession number 25544-26044). Tagore telegrammed Mussolini after receiving the books and it read "Allow me to convey to you cordial appreciation of Indian civilization, and deputing Prof Tucci of the University of Rome for acquainting our scholars with Italian history and culture and working with us in various departments of oriental studies and also for the generous gift of books in your name, showing magnanimity of the tradition of your great country"[21]. Similarly, the library received books as gifts from Government of Mysore (1927), Osmania University (1929), Pramatha Choudhury, Satish Chandra Bagchi, Humayan Kabir, to name only a few. Thus from its very inception the library system in Visva Bharati developed as knowledge centre with direct inspiration and contribution of Rabindranath Tagore and generous contributions from celebrated scholars.

Tagore in his numerous writings mentions the role of library to create an atmosphere of generating and nurturing of knowledge. In his speech as Chairman of reception Committee of All India Libraries Association, Tagore warned librarians as to the passion of numbers (i.e. big collection building}. He declares, "Greed is one of the men's chief internal enemies. Once he starts to gather and store, he becomes distresses with the obsession on numbers, and tends to overlook the purpose of his accumulating… most libraries are possessed with this passion for accumulation. Three-quarter of their books do not come into use—their overgrown proportions…"

For effective use of thought content in library collection he remarked "That part of its contents which is for the purpose of extensive accumulation has its usefulness, but the other part which is for constant and vivid use, gives it its significance." To ensure fullest use of the library Tagore suggests, "it is necessary that its contents should be clearly and specifically brought to notice" with human touch as catalogue has no introduction, no invitation, no spirit of welcome. He reminds "that the readers makes the library, it is not the whole truth; the library likewise makes the readers". It is true as the librarian bridges the gap between the reader and his/her document. However, "its invitation should be active. For, as the Sanskrit proverb goes; *tannashtam yannadiyate*, that which is not given is wasted"[22].

In his institution Tagore wanted to create "the atmosphere of ideas". For that reason he recommended copious free reading by children from the literature in the mother tongue. He also desired that some amount of "rapid reading" should be encouraged in other language as well, like English and Sanskrit, so that plenty of words, expressions and ideas may be assimilated through the subconscious process[23]. Library as knowledge centre can create such an atmosphere "where the mind is without fear and the head is held high; where knowledge is free"[24].

Cultural Functions and Festivals

Tagore laid special emphasis on the importance of knowledge and assimilation of the essential culture and scholarship of one's own country. He believed "culture can accomplish the faculties of mind from the deepest core. A cultured man becomes spontaneously successful from within. Through the influence of culture, man naturally possesses a determined love for knowledge and dispassionate encouragement for activity"[25]. That is why Tagore introduced a number of cultural functions and festivals in his educational experiment to establish a bond between education and society with the objective of full development of human personality through the exchange of ideas, ideals and attitudes. To quote him again "Truth reveals itself through the communion and integration between man and man. A festival is worth the name which we realize the truth of union." Again "The truth that lies in the Union is not mere a scientific knowledge, it is joy, it is life, it is love. It is not fractional but integral whole, because it helps perfection not only of our intellect, but also of our feelings and emotions"[26]. Accordingly Tagore introduces several annual festivals like Spring festival (*Vasanta Utsava*), Ploughing festival (*Hala Karsa Utsava*), Planting festival (*Briksha Ropan Utsava*), Industrial festival (*Shilpa Utsava*), Autumn festival, *Poush Utsava* and *Magh Utsava*. These festivals provide a platform for communication and integration, and exchange of knowledge between the educands, educator and masses.

The Spring festival is observed to expose learners to Nature and make them conscious about its colourful change. In these festivals pupils through their music and dance recitals welcome various seasons like Spring and Autumn. It is expected that the community would share the feelings of communion of man with nature. The philosophy behind celebration of these festivals is to modernize *Tapovan* ideals. Likewise through Plowing and Industrial festivals. Tagore wanted to dignify these professions and life of the persons who are at work in agriculture, craft and industry. Celebration of these festivals helps to make the society conscious about the need of the involvement of the educated people in the field of agriculture, craft and industry. To dignify plowing, Tagore himself plowed the land in the first Plowing festival. To highlight cultivation a respectful profession Tagore wrote "Cultivation of land gave birth to the co-operation between man and man... In the stairs of civilization, cultivation followed the discovery of fire... Applied agriculture liberated greatly human society from the narrow limits of personal selfishness and made possible the union of many people of the society by a bond of livelihood"[27]. Through the Plantation festival, Tagore wanted to develop environmental awareness among people as plantation helps in preventing soil erosion, purification and beautification of the atmosphere, increasing fertility of the soil and also meeting the needs of woods.

Tagore introduced two more important festivals, *Poush Utsava* and *Magh Utsava* for communion and integration between man and man at local, regional and even national level. Tagore observed, "according to us poverty problem is not so important. It is the problem of unhappiness, that is the great problem"[28]. To organize *Magh Utsava* he wrote to Elmhirst, "I hope, you will establish an annual *Mela* (fair) of your own at Surul and encourage the holding of lantern lecturers and games during it as well as the usual dramas and dance"[29]. Thus exhibition, film show, folk songs, folk dance, open theatres, philosophical and literary symposiums are organized every year to communicate latest knowledge, develop social awareness among people, impart mass education through projection of Indian culture. Tagore tried to develop a need-based life-centered knowledge generation and dissemination system through celebration of various functions and festivals as they help bring the institution close to the community breaking the barrier between the elite and the folk.

Rural Reconstruction

Tagore expressed his first-hand rural experience as "...the sorrow and poverty of the villages became clear to me, and I began to grow restless to do something about it...from that time forward I continually endeavoured to find out how villagers' mind could be aroused, so that they themselves could accept responsibility of their own lives"[30]. The ideas took concrete shape with the establishment of Sriniketan (Abode of Lakshmi) in November 1921. To start with the reconstruction programme, survey was conducted to gather information on socio-economic problems. The result of this survey indicated the problem of ignorance and disease as well as the problem of communication of knowledge to the illiterate villagers. The underlying principle was "liberate these few villages in every respect so that all may receive education; a breeze of joy may blow once again; songs and music, recitation from epics and scriptures may fill them, as of yore"[31].

The manifold rural development problems like health, economy, education are interlinked and the rural development programme at Sriniketan attacked them simultaneously. In the words of Elmhirst "from the outset, we had two main objectives, to survey the economic, social and scientific needs of the cultivator in his home, village and fields, and secondly to carry out our laboratory experiments in health, education, craft, cultivation and animal husbandry"[32]. Tagore gave equal importance to health, wealth, knowledge and peace. According to him rural development is only possible if we "bring to the village health and knowledge, wealth and peace in which to live, wealth of time in which to work and to rest and enjoy'[33]. Tagore thought educational development and knowledge communication as foundation of rural development and expressed "reform of education and regeneration of villages are the major tasks of my life"[34].

Tagore was convinced that what the villagers needed for their own salvation was knowledge, a cooperative spirit and encouragement to self-help. To gather as well as to disseminate more practical knowledge, different studies, surveys, experiments were conducted on handloom industry, agriculture, forestry, etc. Sudhir Sen, another director of the institution wrote, "I therefore, launched a study, among other things, of the economics of the handloom industry to determine under what conditions it could be rehabilitated and made not only viable, but also sufficiently profitable"[35]. Later on three research organizations were established namely: Visva-Bharati Economic Research (VER), Social and Economic Planning Association (SEPA), and Indian Society of Agricultural Economics (ISEA) to gather more practical information. The information thus gathered was communicated to the masses mainly through traditional folk education and entertainment. For this Tagore revived traditional rural recreational functions like *jarta, kirtans* and *kathakata* and also introduces different festivals to celebrate seasons.

Conclusion

Tagore's vision of knowledge communication was an integral part of his educational philosophy. The objective of education according to him is "to give man the unity of truth" and "the full realization of all the ideals in the life through work and wisdom"[36]. Tagore tried to translate many of the thoughts into concrete action, for regeneration of the society not only through knowledge generation but also its communication to the masses. For this he took help both of the conventional and non-conventional channels of communication. He believed that an educational institution as a true centre of learning should gather and accumulate knowledge from all parts of the glove, assimilate the same into the body of its own national learning and culture and disseminate it through different channels for the benefit of the nation. Knowledge has a significant decisive role in the realization of individual, national and international goals. So it should be our endeavour to relate education as a unique medium of knowledge generation and dissemination to the real life, needs and aspiration of the people. It is a powerful instrument for the social, economic and cultural transformation necessary for the realization of the social goals. Library as a storehouse of knowledge and an integral part of the present day educational system can help people "who look beyond their books, who have vision, who are seekers, who possesses an all encompassing interest and delight in the direct knowledge of things"[37].

Notes and References

1. Tagore, Rabindranath. Schoolmaster. *Modern Review*. Vol. 36; 1924; p. 313.
2. Tagore, Rabindranath, *Siksha*. Santiniketan: Visva-Bharati, 1352 (B.S.), p. 181.
3. Tagore, Rabindranath, *Personality*. London: Macmillan, 1942, p. 116.
4. Tagore, Rabindranath, *Siksha*. Santiniketan: Visva-Bharati, 1342 (B.S.), p. 152.
5. Tagore, Rabindranath, Sikshar herpher. In *Siksha*. Santiniketan: Visva-Bharati, 1342 (B.S.), p. 6.
6. Tagore, Rabindranath, *Itihas*. Santiniketan: Visva-Bharati, 1362 (B.S.), p. 158.
7. Tagore, Rabindranath, Sikahar svangikaran. In *Siksha*. Santiniketan: Visva-Bharati, 1342 (B.S.), p. 70.
8. Tagore, Rabindranath, Stri-siksha. In *Siksha*. Santiniketan: Visva-Bharati, 1342 (B.S.), p. 18.

9. Tagore, Rabindranath, *Siksha*. Santiniketan: Visva-Bharati, 1352 (B.S.), p. 25.
10. Tagore, Rabindranath, *Siksha*. Santiniketan: Visva-Bharati, 1352 (B.S.), p. 270.
11. Tagore, Rabindranath, *Rashiyar cithi*. Santiniketan: Visva-Bharati, 1363 (B.S.), p. 112.
12. Tagore, Rabindranath, *Sikahar svangikaran*. In *Siksha*. Santiniketan: Visva-Bharati, 1351 (B.S.), p. 15.
13. Tagore, Rabindranath, *Realisation*. London: Macmillan, 1917, p. 53.
14. Tagore, Rabindranath, Sikahar svangikaran. In *Siksha*. Santiniketan: Visva-Bharati, 1351 (B.S.), p. 319-20.
15. *Visva-Bharati Belletin*. (11); 1928; p. 1.
16. *Visva-Bharati*. 1358 (B.S.), (7th Poush), p. 122.
17. Tagore, Rabindranath. *Siksha*. Calcutta: Visva-Bharati Granthan Vibhaga, 1973, p. 18.
18. Tagore, Rabindranath, *Santiniketan Brahmacaryasram*. Visva-Bharati, 1358 (B.S.) (7th Poush).
19. Tagore, Rabindranath, *Santiniketan adiparba*. *Visva-Bharati Patrika*, 1349 (B.S.).
20. *Visva-Bharati Annual Report*, 1922.
21. Mukhopadhyaya, Prabhatkumar. *Rabindrajivani*. Vol. 3, Calcutta: Visva-Bharati Granthan Vibhaga, 1961, p. 249.
22. Tagore (Rabindranath). *Librarir Mukhya Kartabya*. Tagore as Chairman of the Reception Committee of All India Libraries Association prepared this speech in Dec. 1928. Due to his illness Mr. Hirendranath Dutta read out the speech. It appeared in *Indian Library Journal*. Vol. 11 (2-4); 1929.
23. *Visva-Bharati Patrika*, 1349 (B.S.), (Agrahayana), p. 295-6.
24. Tagore, Rabindranath. *Gitanjali* (Bilingual Edition). Santiniketan: Rabindra-Bhavana, 1999, p. 86.
25. Tagore, Rabindranath, *Siksha*. Santiniketan: Visva-Bharati, 1935, p. 226.
26. Tagore, Rabindranath, *Rabindra rachanavali*. Calcutta: Govt. of West Bengal, 1961, p. 5.
27. Tagore, Rabindranath, *Palli Prakriti*. Calcutta: Visva-Bharati Granthan Vibhaga, 1962, pp. 106-7.
28. Elmhirst (L.K.). *The Robbery of the Soil*. Lecture delivered by L.K. Elmhirst, first Director of Sriniketan (Institute of Rural Reconstruction) at Rammohun Roy Library, on 28th July1922. Published in *Modern Review*, Oct. 1922.

29. Tagore, Rabindranath, *Diary*. Dated 4th Dec. 1921.
30. Extracts from the talk delivered by Tagore to Sriniketan workers in summer 1939, later translated into English by Marjorie Sykes and first published in *Modern an Review*, Nov. 1941.
31. Tagore (Rabindranath). *Ibid.*
32. Elmhirst, L.K., *Poet and plowman*. Calcutta: Visva-Bharati Granthan Vibhaga, 1975, p. 48.
33. Tagore, Rabindranath. *City and Village*. Calcutta: Visva-Bharati Granthan Vibhaga, 1973, p. 116.
34. Tagore, Rabindranath, *Rabindra Rachanavali*, Calcutta: Govt. of West Bengal, 1961, p. 582.
35. Sen, Sudhir, *Rabindranath on rural reconstruction*. Calcutta: Visva-Bharati Granthan Vibhaga, 1991, p. 21.
36. Tagore, Rabindranath. *Personality*. London: Macmillan, 1959, p. 26.
37. Tagore, Rabindranath, *Siksha*. Santiniketan: Visva-Bharati, 1351 (B.S), p. 31.

—

Two

Knowledge Dissemination in Tagore's Model of Rural Reconstruction: An Overview

Introduction

Rabindranath was sent to look after his family property at Silaidaha and Patisar (now in Bangladesh) around December 1880 when he was 19 years. There he acquired first hand experience about the socio-economic conditions of rural Bengal. Many years later, referring to those early experiences of village life, Tagore wrote "People used to come with their joys and sorrows, their claims and complaints. All these enabled me to form a true picture of villages. The outward appearance with rivers and wide plains, rice fields and huts nestling in the shelter of trees became familiar to me as also the inner story of rural life. The sufferings of the people became more and more intertwined with my daily work". He continued, "gradually the sorrow and poverty of the villages became clear to me, and I began to grow restless to do something about it… from that time forward I continually endeavoured to find out how villagers mind could be aroused, so that they themselves could accept responsibility for their own lives"[1]. From his first experience Tagore realized that the villagers had lost the ability to help themselves and both research and technical assistance (for dissemination of research results) were necessary even to teach them how to rescue themselves from their decay.

Tagore purchased a house and land at Sural[2] of Birbhum district from Lord S.P. Sinha of Raipur in 1912 which formed the nucleus of his rural reconstruction programmme. The house was in need of repairs and was surrounded by jungles. "It was clearly a deadly breeding place for malarial mosquitoes"[3]. The idea could not take shape until Mr. Elmhirst[4] arrived at Santiniketan (Abode of Peace) in November 1921 and later took charge of Sriniketan (Abode of Lakshmi) as its first director. Thus, Sriniketan started its activity with the direct involvement of three great personalities—Tagore, with his vision and dreams; Elmhirst with his leadership, sympathy and love for poor villagers of Bengal and Mrs. Straight[5] with her gift of money.

The programme started with a general survey of rural life and proper investigation into the economic and social problems of village life. The question of ignorance and diseases were addressed and solution to the problem of dissemination of knowledge to the villagers sought. The information thus gathered was utilized as an essential tool for decision-making before the real work started. The underlying principle was "we must liberate these few villages in every respect so that all may receive education, a breeze of joy may blow once again, songs and music, recitation from epics and scriptures may fill them, as of yore. Mould just these few villages…"[6]. The main objective of this rural reconstruction programme according to its creator was "to try to flood the chocked bed of village life with the stream of happiness". To fulfill this objective Tagore appealed to "the scholars, the poets, the musicians, the artists to collaborate, to offer their contributions"[7].

Birbhum

When Tagore took up the programme of rural reconstruction, Birbhum district was a backward region with the village conditions worse than most other district of Bengal. The soil was of very poor quality, being of red laterite desert (known as *khowai*), and the land was eroded by rain for miles because of deforestation. The peasantry was poorer and more backward compared to their counterparts in other districts. Physically also, the people were off-colour as malaria joined hands with other social and economic evils. Various small trades and crafts of the villages were gradually driven out by big industries. The condition of the region was well summed up by its first director as "when Tagore handed over to us his farm at the village of Surul in the Birbhum district, as the basis of our operations for the founding of a School of Agriculture and the study of village economics, we were compelled to examine not merely the conditions of the soil around us, but the history, social, economic and political aspects which lay behind that condition. The press is constantly giving you strategies showing the increasing death rate, the all powerful sway of malaria and disease, the grinding poverty and the frequency of famine in this area"[8].

Recognizing the importance of information as the basic input for planning proper rural development strategy, a survey was conducted in the village of Ballavpur in 1926. The survey classified 24 families as shown in Table 2.1[9].

Almost all the people including the Brahmins were engaged in agriculture. Paddy was the main crop; potatoes and sugarcane were also cultivated. The total area of the village was 3,744 bighas (about 1,500 acres) which was divided as shown in Table 2.2.

Table 2.1: Categories of People

Higher Castes		*Backward Castes*	
Categories	*Family(ies)*	*Categories*	*Family(ies)*
Brahmins	6	Tanners	7
Weavers	3	Hadis	2
Potters	1	Doms	3
Barbers	1		
Tamils	1		

Table 2.2: Area of Various Types of Land

Area	*Bigha(s)**
Wasteland and *Khowai* (eroded)	2,748.36
Homesteads	42.00
Tanks	42.00
Fallow and left out grazing	201.00
Under Cultivation	457.00
Other lands	255.64

*One acre = about 2.5 bighas

About one hundred bighas of land could be brought under cultivation. Twenty-three out of twenty-four families were in debt expecting the tanner family which was debt free.

Tagore's Model of Rural Reconstruction

Tagore realized that problem of rural reconstruction were manifold and the problems related to health, economy, education, etc., are interlinked with each other. So all the problems were to be attacked at a time, instead of dealing with them in isolation. The objectives of the programme, in the words of Elmhirst evolved as follows: "from the outset, we had two main objectives, to survey the economic, social and scientific needs of the cultivator in his home, village and fields, and secondly to carry out our own laboratory experiments in health, education, craft, cultivation and animal husbandry"[10]. Tagore gave equal importance to health, wealth, knowledge and peace. According to him rural upliftment is only possible if we "bring to the village health and knowledge, wealth and peace in which to live, wealth of time in which to work and to rest and enjoy"[11].

Accordingly Tagore laid emphasis on economy (with special emphasis on agriculture and local handicraft), education, health, village organization, research and training and also on different methods in knowledge communication mainly based on traditional folklore of Bengal. Regarding economic development Tagore's aspiration "was to make the cultivator self-confident in his own ability..." and he felt that "the right of agricultural lands should vest with the peasants... There cannot be real improvement of agriculture unless we adopt collective and co-operative farming on scientific lines"[12]. Tagore considered educational development as foundation of rural reconstruction and "reform of education and regeneration of villages are the major tasks of my life"[13]. The poet furthered observed "a natural bond between education in the schools and colleges and the country outside them is immensely necessary"[14].

The village welfare department of the institute from the very beginning took the programme of health and sanitation in the surrounded villages. In the year 1929, the institute treated 6760 patients[15]. Tagore firmly believed that poverty, disease, depopulation, joylessness and backwardness of rural area could be removed only through co-operative efforts of village organization. "I pray for the victory of the co-operative principles" the poet wrote from Soviet Russia in 1930. Sriniketan from the very beginning laid special emphasis on research, training and knowledge communication which is expressed in its objectives reproduced below:

1. To take the problem of the villages and the field to the classroom for study and discussion and to experimental farm for solution.
2. To carry the knowledge and experience gained in the classroom and farm to the villagers in their endeavours to improve their sanitation and health; to develop their resources and credit; to help them to sell their product and buy their requirements to the best advantages; to teach them better methods of growing crops, and vegetables and of keeping livestock; to encourage them to learn and practice art and crafts; and to bring home to them the benefits of associated life, mutual aid and common endeavour[16].

The model is presented in Fig. 2.1.

Knowledge Dissemination

According to Tagore "knowledge is the greatest factor of unity among human beings". Through knowledge one became conscious of human unity, which transcends difference of time and space. Learning about its utility, no one should be deprived of the joy that issues from the consciousness of this unity"[17]. Tagore always laid emphasis on importance of information. In his address before the students of Srinikatan in 1905 he appealed to them to assist the Bengal Literary Society in gathering information on poems, songs, folklore, ruins of temples, old manuscripts, village festivals, religious scriptures, method of cultivation, etc., in order to discover our

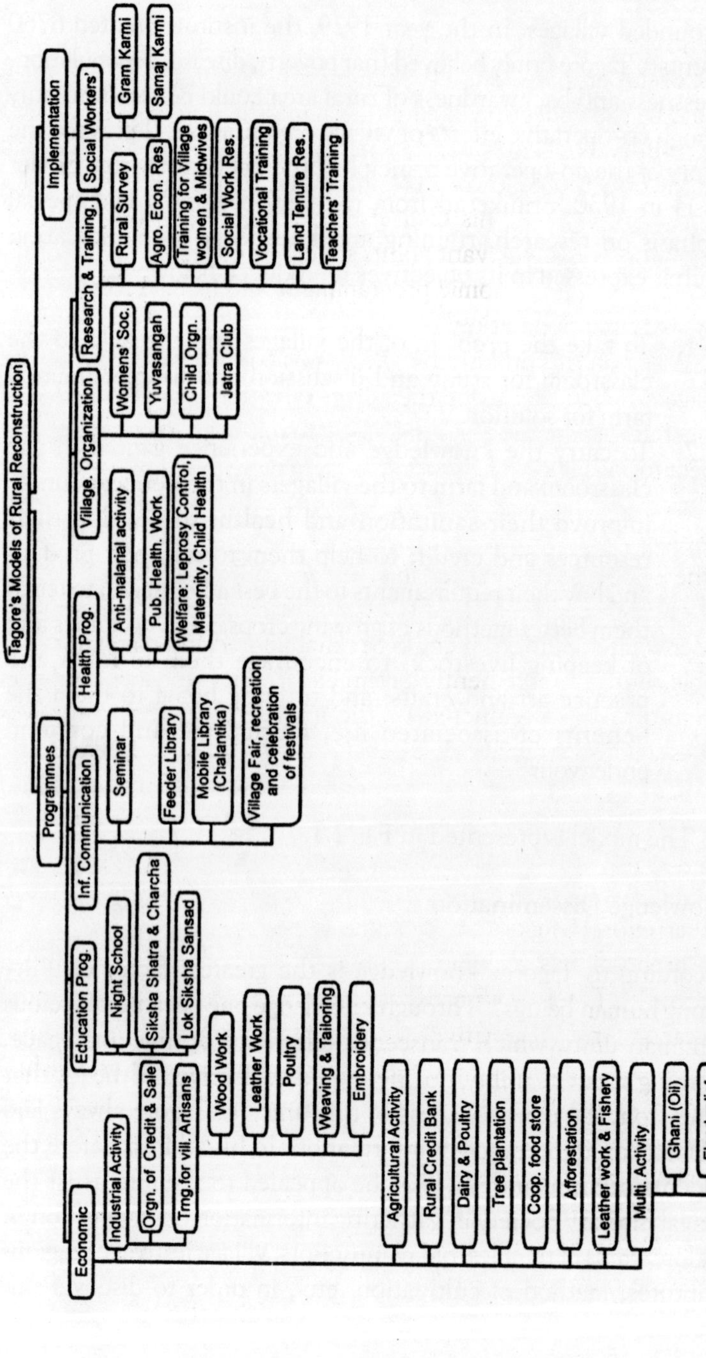

Fig. 2.1: Model of Rural Reconstruction

country"[18]. Again in Pabna address in 1907 he urged that the first task of the proposed rural branches of the Provincial Conference would be the collection of all kinds of information in every part of the country. For "knowledge is a necessary prelude to action". And it is the only tool to know the conditions prevailing in real field of work.[19] Similarly, in his *Call of Truth*, Tagore insisted that full information on all relevant points should be collected first in order to decide which economic programme would be best to meet the needs of rural population[20].

Based on this philosophy Tagore was convinced that what the villagers needed most for their own salvation was knowledge, a cooperative spirit and encouragement to self-help. Recognizing this aspect to gather as well as to disseminate more practical knowledge different studies, surveys, experiments were conducted on handloom industry, agriculture, etc. Sudhir Sen, another director of the institute wrote "I therefore launched on a study, among other things, of the economics of the handloom industry to determine under what conditions it could be rehabilitated and made not only viable, but also sufficiently profitable"[21]. An intensive study on agriculture was conducted by the institute and the result was published in a volume called *Land and its Problem*[22]. To green the earth, to bind the soil and conserve moisture of Sriniketan and nearby villages, Sen conducted a study of trees of the compound of Mr. Cheap "made an inventory of all the trees, by species and number, which were still standing in the compound and suggested that an effort be made to reforest the whole place... The idea behind the proposal was to build a miniature forest for demonstration purpose"[23]. Later on in order to encourage the problem-oriented research and planning and to help economic and social development in India, three research organizations were established namely: Visva Bharati Economic Research (VER), Social and Economic Planning Association (SEPA), and Indian Society of Agricultural Economics (ISAE). Knowledge is not an end but a means to an end. Theoretical knowledge is not enough, it is to be communicated and shared. Subjective knowledge becomes complete only when learning in brought down from the realm of abstraction to the world of concrete experience. To disseminate knowledge Tagore not only laid emphasis on seminar, library, research ad training but also on fairs and festivals, recreation and village organization. Tagore observes, "according to us poverty problem is not so important. It is the problem of unhappiness hat is the great problem"[24].

In this context he wrote to Elmhirst "I hope, you will establish an annual *mela* (fair) of your own at Surul and encourage the holding of lantern lectures and games during it as well as the usual dramas and dance"[25]. As a result, agricultural fair at Sriniketan started. To disseminate information the institute also took part in other fairs of the district. The diary of Elmhirst dated 10th February 1922 reads "tomorrow we pack up and all leave to attend the annual *mela* (fair and agricultural show and demonstration combined) at Suri, Birbhum district headquarters. At 8.30 a.m. I was round to the tents and then the boys to the Mela, or Fairground…There we were able to fix up a most interesting programme, trips to local sugarcane plots, demonstration in tanning, weaving and silk culture, with peanut oil extraction as well, and with lectures as well on veterinary science, hygiene and agriculture, and from officers of the Bengal Government"[26]. Organisation of regular lectures was a part of the activities of the institute. "The second lecture on our local problem is finished. The poet keeps pestering me to get the first one into final shape so that he can translate it into Bengali"[27]. In 1929 twenty-six such lectures were delivered in nineteen villages, with a total attendance of 6,000 people[28].

Tagore laid emphasis on extension of education through folk education and folk entertainment. He believed that only through folklore i.e. through traditional culture we could be able to plough back our stored knowledge into the soil of mass mind. For this reason Tagore revived traditional rural recreational functions like *jatra* (an open-air opera performance), *kirtan* (act of singing the names of God), *kathakatha* (act of narration of scriptural and mythological stories), etc, and organized different festivals to celebrate various seasons. e.g. *varshamangal* to celebrate rainy season. He believed that "culture can accomplish the faculties of mind from the deepest core. A cultured man becomes spontaneously successful from within...Through the influence of culture man naturally possess a disinterested love for knowledge and a dispassionate encouragement for activity"[29]. "Knowledge associated with joy and satisfaction increases our power of learning, consequently our power of reception, apprehension, thinking and judgement develop easily and naturally"[30].

Education is the greatest instrument for purposeful dissemination of knowledge in village life. Tagore laid emphasis on the education of village boys and girls. The poet believed that the success of entire rural reconstruction scheme depended upon them as they were the future leaders of knowledge generation and dissemination. For this the institute established various formal and non-formal educational wings like night school, *Siksha Satra, Siksha Charcha*, etc. The poet stated, "reform of education and regeneration of villages are the major tasks of my life"[31]. According to him the objective of education is the full realization of all ideals in life through work and wisdom as "the highest education is that which does not give us information but makes our life harmony with all existence"[32].

Present Activity for Rural Reconstruction

With the passage of time Sriniketan laid greater emphasis on new programmes of rural education and extension keeping in view the changing socio-economic scenario. The idea is to encourage the villagers to become self-reliant through formation of Self-Help Group, Youth Organisation, *Mahila Samities* (Ladies Club), etc. Presently, the Institute follows the U.G.C. guidelines of 1998 and 1992, i.e. the area-based approach to rural education and extension. The present operational area of Rural Extension Centre is diagrammatically represented as in Fig. 2.2.

The present activities of Rural Extension Centre include the following broad areas based on Tagore's model of rural reconstruction and knowledge dissemination. These activities are:

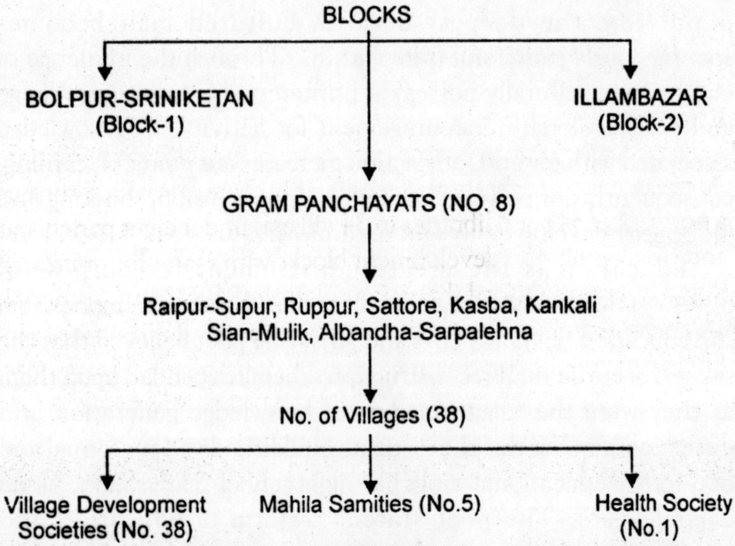

Fig. 2.2: Functions of Rural Extension Centre

1. Broti Balak Programme
2. Rural Library Programme
3. Innovative Community Learning Programme
4. Self-Help Group
5. Adult Education Programme
6. Continuing Education Programme
7. Women and Child Welfare Programme
8. Women Empowerment Programme
9. Training Programme
10. Agricultural Extension
11. Games and Sports
12. Promotion of *Rabindrasangeet* (Tagore Song)
13. Promotion of Art and Culture
14. Promotion of Folk Culture
15. Awareness Programme
16. Economic Development Programme
17. Health Extension

18. Environmental Education
19. Day's Celebration[33]

Rural Library

At present Rural Library Services (2011-12) are provided through a network of 34 rural libraries in 34 villages under eight panchayats and two community development blocks with matching grant from Raja Rammohum Roy Library Foundation (RRRLF) to strengthen library programme. The objectives of the Rural Library Programme (including mobile library) are:

- Develop the reading habits among villagers
- Use library as a cultural, communication and continuing education centre
- Develop self-reliance and self-confidence
- Provide all updated information regarding modern and advanced science and technology
- Retention of acquired literacy skill
- Development of knowledge power
- Development of cultural sense among people
- Development of habits for exchanging ideas and views
- Development of science–tempered readers society.

The Mobile Library Unit of the institute organizes regular meeting, exhibition, and competition among readers, library visit, and book collection drive from villagers as gift to library.

Conclusion

On the basis of the experience of rural life and analysis of the causes of poverty, Tagore showed the real path of rural reconstruction. He insisted on mass contact for knowledge dissemination; emphasized the need for cooperative activities for the solution of India's grave economic problem, and urged people to utilize traditional rural institutions like *melas* (fairs), and *jatras* (open air opera performance) for rousing popular consciousness and mass entertainment. Sriniketan was Tagore's project of rural reconstruction as he observed "I cannot single –handedly bear the responsibility for the whole of India. I shall conquer only one or two tiny villages. But if I can liberate two or three villages from the bondage of ignorance and incapacity, then on a small scale the idea would be established for the whole of India"[34]. Now in independent India the responsibility Tagore took upon himself has devolved on the shoulders of the Government particularly after 74th constitutional amendment to spread democracy at grassroots level.

In addition to the first hand experience by Tagore for the development of the rural community, we can add some basic objectives for the development of rural community and help them for lifelong self-education; and contribution to productivity by informing from top state level management to lower level management. The basic objective in Indian context should be to assist the general people to acquire knowledge for their personal development and social well-being and contribute to the communication of already generated knowledge for promoting the society and the nation as a whole.

Notes and References

1. Extracts taken from the talk delivered by the poet to Sriniketan workers in summer 1939, later translated into English by Marjorie Sykes and first published in *Modern Review* (Nov. 1941)
2. Later named Sriniketan (Institute of Rural Reconstruction), name suggested by Leonard K. Elmhirst and duly approved by Rabindranath Tagore.
3. Andrews, C.F. *Rabindranath Tagore*. Santiniketan: Santiniketan Press.
4. K. Elmhirst Leonard Graduated from Cambridge and studied agriculture at Cornell University.
5. Elmhirst joined Sriniketan with funds provided by Mrs. Straight, later she became Mrs. Elmhirst.
6. Tagore, Rabindranath. Sriniketan address. *Modern Review*. 1941 (Nov.).

7. Tagore, Rabindranath. *City and Village*. Santiniketan: Visva Bharati, 1976, p. 24.
8. The Robbery of the Soil, lecture delivered by L.K. Elmhirst at the Rammohun Library, 28th July 1922. Rabindranath Tagore presided over the meeting. First published in *Modern Review*. Oct 1922.
9. Survey conducted by the Institute and edited by Kali Mohan Ghosh, a social worker of Sriniketan.
10. Elmhirst, Leonard K. *Poet and Plowman*. Santiniketan: Visva Bharati, 1976, p. 48.
11. Tagore, Rabindranath. *City and Village*. Santiniketan: Visva Bharati, 1976, p. 116.
12. Tagore, Rabindranath. *Siksha*. Santiniketan: Visva Bharati, 1961, p. 330. Tr. by the author.
13. Tagore, Rabindranath. *Rabindra-Rachanavali*. Calcutta: Govt. of West Bengal, 1961, p. 582.
14. Tagore, Rabindranath. *Siksha*. Santiniketan: Visva Bharati, 1973, p. 20. Tr. by the author.
15. Lal, Premchand. *Reconstruction and Education in Rural India*. London: George Allen and Unwin, 1932, p. 78.
16. Tagore, Rabindranath. *Visva Bharati Bulletin*. 11; 1928; p. 1.
17. Tagore, Rabindranath. *Sikshar Bahan*. Santiniketan: Visva Bharati, 1973, p. 12.
18. Tagore, Rabindranath. *Siksha*. Santiniketan: Visva Bharati, 1961, pp. 32-33.
19. Tagore, Rabindranath. *Samuha*. Santiniketan: Visva Bharati,1961, p. 97.
20. Tagore, Rabindranath. *Satyer Ahwan* (Call of Truth). *Kalantar;* 1344 (BS); p. 173.
21. Sen, Sudhir. *Rabindranath on Rural Reconstruction*. Santiniketan: Visva Bharati, 1991, p. 21.
22. Sen, Sudhir. *Land and its Problem*. Santiniketan: Visva Bharati, 1943, p. 49.
23. Sen, Sudhir. *Op. cit.* p. 19.
24. Elmhirst, L.K., *The Robbery of the Soil*. Lecture delivered at Rammohun Roy Library, 28th July 1922. Introduction by Rabindranath Tagore. *Modern Review*. 1922 (October).
25. Elmhirst, L.K. *Diary*, dated 4 December 1921.
26. Elmhirst, L.K. *Diary*, dated 10 February 1922.
27. Elmhirst, L.K. *Diary*, dated 25 February 1922.
28. Lal, Premchand. *Reconstruction and Education in Rural India*. London: George Allen & Unwin, 1932, pp. 82-83.

29. Tagore, Rabindranath. *Siksha*. Santiniketan: Visva Bharati, 1973, p. 226. Tr. by the author.
30. *Ibid*. p. 8.
31. Tagore, Rabindranath. *Rabindra-Rachanavali*. Calcutta: Govt. of West Bengal, 1961.
32. Tagore, Rabindranath. *Personality*. London: Macmillan, 1959, p. 116.
33. *Annual Report*. 2007-08. Sriniketan: Rural Extension Centre, Visva-Bharati.
34. Tagore, Rabindranath. *Sriniketan Address*. *Modern Review*. 1941 (November).

Three

Tagore's Vision of Library: A Study

Introduction

The writings of Rabindranath Tagore are universal in expression and temper but rooted in oriental culture. His writings on literature, music, art, education, rural development, history, cooperative ideas, etc, in one hand and on the other hand his activities on experimental school at Santiniketan, rural reconstruction programme at Sriniketan, all turned into gold with the passage of time. This is true in case of Tagore's vision of library in his writings as well as its implementation at Santiniketan.

Tagore's numerous writings on 'library' touches every aspect of library science right from collection development, documentation, conservation, to the effective use of collection. Tagore's vision was to establish Visva-Bharati as a centre of universal culture and research *'Yatra visvam bhavatyekenidam'* (where the world makes its home in a single nest). The objective of development of education and library is clearly expressed in the trust deed made by Maharshi Devendranath Tagore, father of Rabindranath Tagore in the year 1888 which reads as follows: "in pursuance of the need of enhancement of the quality of living in the Ashram the trustees were empowered to establish a Brahmavidyalaya at Santiniketan and a library"[1]. Thus the concept of library was from the very beginning a constituent of the Santiniketan Ashram. Tagore wrote,

"The collection of our revered father's books was kept in one of the three rooms. We first looked after the proper preservation of books and manuscripts. What occupied our thoughts thereafter was where we could fix students' residence"[2]. Tagore's writings and growth of Visva-Bharati and its library are linked with the growth of his life as he wrote "the growth of this school was the growth of my life and not of a mere carrying out of my doctrines, its ideals changed with the maturity like a ripening fruit that not only grows in its bulk and deepens in its colour, but undergoes change in the very quality of its inner pulp"[3].

Tagore's Vision of Library: A Theoretical Approach

Tagore's writings on book and library cover both philosophical and functional aspect of library science. In two essays namely "Library"[4] and "Librarir Mukhyo Kartabyo"[5] Rabindranath expressed his philosophical and functional vision of a library. The first one covers the philosophical aspects where Tagore described library as a place where sounds of ocean of thousand years stopped like a sleeping child, flow of language; currents are imprisoned by the chain of black words. People get a chance to move in any direction of knowledge. Rabindranath describes library as a place where man encompasses his freedom in a small place. In the functional aspect he advised librarians to be free from bias of the number of accumulating as "once he starts to gather and store, he becomes distracted with the obsession of number, and tends to overlook the purpose of his accumulating." "The part of its contents which is for the purpose of extensive accumulation has its usefulness, but the other part which is for constant and varied use, gives its significance"[6]. In respect of documentation Rabindranath suggested "it is necessary that its contents should be clearly and specifically brought to notice. Otherwise it is very difficult for the ordinary man to find his way about them, and the library is left as a city of vast accommodation that lacks means of communication"[7]. Rabindranath in his poem has mentioned that books may be kept in precious racks with good care, but without proper use it is meaningless[8].

For developing readership in a library Rabindranath reminds that the readers make the library is not the whole truth; but library also makes readers. For this, library has to go beyond the traditional form of invitation "Here is my catalogue, come and select for yourself". "But in the usual catalogue there is no introduction, no invitation, and no spirit of welcome. That library alone can be called hospitable, which shows an eagerness to invite readers to the feast at its disposal, it is such hospitability that makes a library big not its size"[9]. As to the role of a librarian Rabindranath suggests "the worth of a librarian I would gauge by his power of attracting and looking after such circle, of acting as the intermediary for an intimacy of relationship between the reader and the library"[10]. Regarding librarian's duty Rabindranath reminds "...as to the books, the librarian's duty should not be confined to those that he can gather, but he must also keep himself acquainted with all those others that are published from time to time, subject by subject"[11].

Tagore in his numerous writings mentioned the role of a library in the development of a society and methods of knowledge communication citing examples from *Sruti* and *Tapabon*[12] and medium of writing from the period of ancient India i.e. Ashok's inscription[13] even with proper example from Greece and Persia[14]. For development of reading habit among school students Rabindranath suggested for rapid reading literature books in English, Sanskrit along with traditional step by step teaching methods in these subjects[15]. For this rapid reading on many subjects, library is the only place. Pramathanath Bisi recaptured his memory of Rabindranath's opinion about library that people can never be truly educated from colleges and teachers, on the other hand he should be the teacher of his own and library is the proper place of education as he learns many things only from huge reading in a library[16]. For development of personal reading Rabindranath also mentioned in his poem that one college student prepares a list of gifts for his beloved one where 'recent fiction' and book of poem 'printed on antique paper' gets it place[17]. The same kind of reference can also be cited from his famous novel *Naukadubi* where Akshay presented books to Hemnalini as gift[18].

A good book is a good friend that helps to know many unknown things, character building and also helps to increase creativity. Besides, it provides many information as it is not possible to go everywhere to observe everything. This concept has been reflected in a poem *Janmadine*[19]. Enhancement of knowledge helps to achieve greater mental satisfaction as well as pleasure[20]. The role of a book as a friend with whom one can exchange ideas has been reflected in a letter of Rabindranath where he mentioned *Amiel's Journal* as an intimate friend[21]. Rabindranath was a voracious reader who became deeply involved with the character of the books he read as he mentioned in describing the episode of *Ramayana* reading in *Jivansmriti*[22]. A good book has a long-term impact on reader's mind like classical song. It has also been reflected in Rabindranath's poetry[23] as well as letters[24]. Good books help to generate new ideas to write new things as Rabindranath has mentioned being impressed by a book entitled *Chineman Letter.* Rabindranath wrote an essay on this[25]. Actually Rabindranath's literary culture starts with habit of reading as he mentioned in *Jivansmriti*[26].

Rabindranath in his writings also warns against to be too much bookish which may create hindrance in the development of imagination and power of expression. Children may loose the power of free mixing by too much reading. He knows the character of books but not the man in his locality. Even this may lead to develop some ideas which have no connection with reality[27]. Rabindranath gave example of this type of detachment. By studying ethnology one tries to learn many things but forgets to be familiar with the neighbor. We consider a book as a real big thing but forget the real people who are described in the book[28].

The success of a library depends on reader satisfaction in pursuit of information or knowledge. Librarians have to be very careful regarding reader's requirement, likeness, reading habit, in a word, reader's psychology. Rabindranath in his numerous writings mentioned these aspects. Truth centered on humanity gets reflected in literature. Only permanent truth can give more satisfaction to readers[29]. The reading habit of different reader varies. Some want to study alone in a lonely place[30]. Married women used to keep books under a pillow to keep them safe from their kids. This is also mentioned in a poem of *Kshanika*[31]. In a poem called *Sisu* Rabindranath has also drawn a picture of *Ramayana* reading in the noon[32]. Such example is also found in the fiction *Chokher Bali* where Binodini is requested to read *Santisatak* for Pishima[33]. The change of reading material from *Ramayana* to modern literature and its likings, and also the picture of a good library of Abinash have been narrated in *Sesher Kavita*[34]. For reader's satisfaction a library should collect best books covering all aspects of reader's requirement. Rabindranath in a letter mentioned this aspect[35].

One of the most important functions of a library is conservation of library collection to keep the documents safe from harm or loss, damage, destruction or decay, and maintain it in reasonably sound condition for present and future use. Rabindranath in his two poems *Kiter Bichar* and *Granthakit*[36] describes the nature of *kit* (worm) and how they destroy book. In the objectives and functions of Santiniketan Brahmacharyasram it is stated that the responsibility of cleaning the library, rooms and garden should be vested to students. Clear instruction was given to collect borrowed books from the guests[37]. In a letter to Subodh Chandra Majumder, Rabindranath's care for book is reflected. Where Rabindranath wrote 'I mailed two books Religious Systems and Origin of Aryans. Keep them in the library. Dust the library and give naphthalene'[38].

Tagore's Writings on Library: A Bibliometric Approach

To conduct the bibliometric study on the concept of library in Tagoreana two major methods were followed:

Literature Survey

Survey is an account of some research examination, or enquiry, which has been done by scientific or organized method. Literature survey is the search for documents including books, journal articles, dissertations, theses, etc. on the subject under research[39]. For literature survey on the subject under study collected works of Rabindranath Tagore[40] as well as all other published and unpublished writings of Tagore and also other probable primary and secondary sources were consulted.

Bibliometric Technique

For bibliometric study, bibliometric technique 'as the quantitative treatment of the properties of recorded discourse and behaviour pertaining to it'[41] was followed. With the help of descriptive bibliometrics, the number of publications in a given year, in different literary form etc. was constructed.

Table 3.1: Number of Publications on Library

Year of Publication	*Number*
1888-1893	2
1893-1898	1
1898-1903	2
1903-1908	3
1908-1913	1
1913-1918	1
1918-1923	1
1923-1928	29
1928-1933	31
1933-1938	2
Total	**76**

Table 3.2: Year-wise Distribution of Publications on Library

Year of Publication	*Number*
1933	22
1931	15
1928	10
1925	7
1923	6
Total	**60**

Table 3.3: Publication on Library in Different Literary Forms

Journal articles	*Letters*	*Addresses*	*Essays*	*Poems*	*Autobiographies*	*Total*
5	12	21	5	29	4	76

Tagore's literary career may be classified as youth and early childhood writings (1878-1900), *Gitanjali* period (1900-1912), the years of matured reflections (1912-1927) and the final years (1927-1941)[42]. Thus from Table 3.1 it is observed that Rabindranath expressed his vision on library throughout his literary career (1883-1938) from childhood writings to final years.

The highest number of writings (N=22) were published in the year 1933, which is 28.95 per cent of total writings on the subject. Rabindranath expressed his vision about library more according to number of publications within 1928-1933 which is 61.84 per cent of total writings. Tagore's presidential address on "*library*" on All India Library Congress 1928 may have some impact on his later writings. He also wrote on functional aspects of library "*Librarir Mukhyo Kartabyo*" (main responsibility of library) in this period. On 76 occasions Rabindranath mentioned the concept of '*Library*' in Tagoreana in all literary forms like letters, addresses, essays, poems, etc. But he wrote mostly on the subject in the form of poems (N = 29, which is 38.16 per cent of total writings) as Rabindranath is predominately a poet.

Rabindranath was eager to develop the library system of India. When he went to Russia he observed the role of a library in academic set up of that country. For the purpose of development of libraries in India, he even compared their system with that India. He mentioned "their museum is not passive like our library at Santiniketan but active"[43]. Today with the advent of education library movement has reached to a point. But one should not forget Rabindranath's remarks—"Establishment of libraries has spread in villages and towns of Bengal. Care should be taken, so that these efforts do not confine to recreation only but can spread culture in public domain"[44].

With this objective of disseminating knowledge to rural mass, Rabindranath started mobile library service.

Genesis of Library Services in Tagore's Visva-Bharati

The site on which the educational institution Visva-Bharati is situated was first purchased in 1863 by Maharshi Debendranath from the Lord Sinhas family of Raipur. Twenty-five years later in 1888, a trust deed was executed by Maharshi Debendranath, father of Rabindranath and the entire site with building and adjacent land was dedicated to the purpose of worship according to "*Brahma*"ideals. The *Asarama* established on 19th October 1888 and a small library came up and started functioning in a room of Santiniketan House. Tagore wrote, "The collection of our revered father's book was kept in one of the three rooms. We first look after the proper preservation of books and manuscripts. What occupied our thought thereafter was where we could fix students"[45].

Before the establishment of the "*Brahmacharyasram*", the boarding school on December 22, 1901, the library was situated in Santiniketan House. But after the establishment of "*Brahmacharyasram*" Rabindranath himself establish *Ashrama* library mainly from his personal collection. He used to receive good number of books as gift from authors and publishers. After going through them Tagore donated the books to library. For that reason now one can find marginal noted wriiten by Tagore in the collection of Visva-Bharati Library.

Tagore's biographer Prabhatkumar Mukhopadhyay (1892-1985) took the responsibility of *Ashrama* library in July 1910. Library started functioning scientifically since then. Library used to receive good number of books as gift all over the world. In the year 1925 library received 500 books from Mousolani of Itali. Acknowledging this gift Tagore wrote him "Allow me to convey to you gratitude in the name of Visva-Bharati for sending us, through Prof. Formichi, your cordial appreciation of Indian civilization and deputing Prof. Tucci of the university of Rome for acquainting our students with Indian history and culture and working with us in various departments of oriental studies and also for the generous gift of books in your name, showing spirit of magnanimity worthy of the tradition of your great country"[46]

The library condition in the yar 1921-22 can be observed from the Annual Report of Visva-Bharati. "The library of Santiniketan is one of the special features of Visva-Bharati. The library posses a very good collection of books on Sanskrit, Pali and Prakrit, a valuable collection of Chinese and Tibetan books. The Indian vernaculars are well presented specially Bengali, Hindi and Gujarati.

It also contains a very unique collection of continental book on Indology and Art, chiefly in French and German. We are indebted for this collection to our friends overseas who have made a free gift of books in this section."[47]. In May 1951 the Parliament of India by Act XXIX of 1951 under the Prime Ministership of Jawaharlal Nehru declared Visva-Bharati as an institute of national importance and provided its functioning as a Unitary, teaching and residential Statutory Central University. Since, then University is receiving regular grants from Central Government and the University is developing in all sphere. Thus the library service in Visva-Bharati is related with the establishment and development of the institute itself.

Besides the library system in the institution the rural library service concept was developed and initiated with the very inception of Sriniketan experiment of rural reconstruction in 1922. Tagore believed that "for the fundamental purpose of education it is not merely to enrich ourselves through the fullness of knowledge, but also to establish the bond of love and friendship between man and man"[48]. For that he suggests "the higher educational institutions should assimilate knowledge from all sources and disseminate it for benefit of the masses in order to strengthen their own foundation"[49]. The same has clearly been stated in one of the objectives of Sriniketan which reads as follows: "to carry the knowledge and experience gained in the class-room and farm to the village"[50]. Rural library services in the form of mobile library services named "Chalantika" started in the year 1925 with an initial collection of 200 books. Now it is functioning in two community development blocks namely Bolpur-Sriniketan and Illambazar covering eight Gram Panchayats of Birbhum district.

Tagore's writings on library and establishment of his experimental school and its library at Santiniketan are based on his educational philosophy of "freedom of mind, freedom of heart and freedom of will"[51]. His idea of a library was alike with his idea of rural development as he states "reform of education and regeneration of villages are the major task of my life"[52]. Tagore gave stress on rural library services as he felt "a natural bond between education in the schools and colleges and the country outside them is immensely necessary"[53]. This is necessary to fulfill the objectives of education as "the highest education is that which does not give us information but makes our life in harmony with all existence"[54]. A library as the storehouse of recorded knowledge has a tremendous role to play. But to ensure fullest use of its resources Tagore suggests, "it is necessary that its contents should clearly and specifically brought to notice" of readers with human touch because "the library by itself imposes a responsibility—the responsibility relating to riches. Insofar as the library contains books, it attains fulfillment only through having those books read. It will not remain inactive; may it play an active role by issuing a call. Because 'Jannastam yanna deeyate' that which is not given is wasted[55].

Conclusion

Tagore's writings on library and establishment of library system at Santiniketan and Sriniketan are based on his educational philosophy of freedom of mind, freedom of heart and freedom of will. According Tagore the objective of education is "to give man unity of truth" and "the full realization of all the ideals in life through work and wisdom"[56]. His idea of library was alike with his idea of rural development "reform of education and regeneration of villages are the major task of my life"[57]. Tagore gave stress on rural library services to establish "a natural bond between education in the schools and colleges and the country outside them..."[58]. This is necessary to fulfill the objectives of education, as "the highest education is that which does not give us information but makes our life in harmony with all existence"[59]. For this library as knowledge centre has a good role to play.

Rabindranath was pioneer in providing mobile library service in India with the establishment of "*Chalantika*" in the year 1925. Dr. Ranganathan also provided mobile library service in Tanjore district of Madras Province with the help of bullock cart, later on he named it '*Librachine*'. For this "MALA (Madras Library Association) had put up a stall at the Park Fair Exhibition of December 1930 at Madras. ...One visitor had made this exhibit worthwhile. It was a sub-engineer in government service one Kanakasabhai Pillai. ....Pillai offered not only to design an appropriate cart with two bullocks, but to finance a vehicle to serve the region around his home-town of Mannargudi, about 40km south-east of Tanjore"[60].

Rabindranath was not only a poet, dramatist, novelist, short story writer, musician, painter, critic, philosopher, educationist, patriot but also a man of action who tried to give his vision a concrete shape with the establishment of his experimental school at Santiniketan and institute of rural development at Sriniketan. Thus, Annada Sankar Ray rightly observed "His life is, in fact" is "Rabindranath's greatest work"[61]. Rabindranath was the 'discoverer and spokesman' of traditional India that is 'basically humanist and universal, simple yet profound'[62]. Thus a study of Tagoreana is only a part of studying the activity of this 'universal man'[63].

Notes and References

1. Tagore, Rabindranath. *Santiniketan brahmacaryasram*. Santiniketan: Visva-Bharati, 1358 (B.S.), p. 26.
2. Tagore, Rabindranath. *Santiniketan adiparba*. Santiniketan: Visva-Bharati, 1349 (B.S.), p. 19.
3. Tagore, Rabindranath. *My school Santiniketan*: 1901-51. Calcutta: Visva-Bharati Granthan Vibhaga, 1951, pp. 6-7.
4. Tagore, Rabindranath. *Vichtra Prabandha*. Calcutta: Visva-Bharati Granthan Vibhaga, 1388 (B.S.), p. 35.
5. Rabindranath as the Chairman of Reception Committee of All India Libraries Association prepared this speech. Due to his illness this was read out by Mr. Hirendranath Dutta. Later it was published in *The Indian Library Journal*, Vol. 2, No. 2-4. 1929.
6. *Ibid.*
7. *Ibid.*
8. Tagore, Rabindranath. *Kshanika*. Calcutta: Visva-Bharati Granthan Vibhaga, 1359 (B.S.), p. 23.
9. Tagore, Rabindranath. *Library and its use. The Indian Library Journal*. 2, 3; 1929; 21-28.
10. *Ibid.*
11. *Ibid.*
12. Tagore, Rabindranath. *Sikshar bikiran: address*. In *Siksha*. Calcutta: Visva-Bharati Granthan Vibhaga, 1405 (B.S.), p. 214.

13. Tagore, Rabindranath. *Sahitya.* Calcutta: Visva-Bharati Granthan Vibhaga, 1398 (B.S.), p. 14.
14. Tagore, Rabindranath. *Japane-Parasha.* Calcutta: Visva-Bharati Granthan Vibhaga, 1343 (B.S.), p. 146.
15. Tagore, Rabindranath. *Siksha.* Santiniketan: Visva-Bharati, 1342 (B.S.), p. 87.
16. Bisi, Pramathanath. *Rabindranath O Santiniketan.* Calcutta: Visva-Bharati Granthan Vibhaga, 1402 (B.S.), p. 129.
17. Tagore, Rabindranath. *Punascha.* Calcutta: Visva-Bharati Granthan Vibhaga, 1372 (B.S.), pp. 13-64.
18. Tagore, Rabindranath. *Naukadubi.* Calcutta: Visva-Bharati Granthan Vibhaga, 1951, p. 160.
19. Tagore, Rabindranath. *Janmadine.* Calcutta: Visva-Bharati Granthan Vibhaga, 1957, p. 20.
20. Tagore, Rabindranath. *Vithika.* Calcutta: Visva-Bharati Granthan Vibhaga, 1351 (B.S.), p. 21.
21. Tagore, Rabindranath. *Chhinapatravali.* Calcutta: Visva-Bharati Granthan Vibhaga, 1367 (B.S.), pp. 251-252.
22. Tagore, Rabindranath. *Jivansmriti.* Calcutta: Visva-Bharati Granthan Vibhaga, 1405 (B.S.), p. 13.
23. Tagore, Rabindranath. *Vithika.* Calcutta: Visva-Bharati Granthan Vibhaga, 1352 (B.S.), pp. 21-23.
24. Tagore, Rabindranath. *Chithipatra.* Vol. 5. Calcutta: Visva-Bharati Granthan Vibhaga, 1352 (B.S.), p. 139.
25. Tagore, Rabindranath. *Rabindra rachanavali.* Vol. 4. Calcutta: Visva-Bharati Granthan Vibhaga, 1385 (B.S.), p. 559.
26. Tagore, Rabindranath. *Jivansmriti.* Calcutta: Visva-Bharati Granthan Vibhaga, 1405 (B.S.), pp. 70-71.
27. Tagore, Rabindranath. *Siksha.* Santiniketan: Visva-Bharati, 1342 (B.S.), pp. 70-71.
28. *Ibid.* pp. 20-25.
29. Tagore, Rabindranath. *Rabindra rachanavali.* Vol. 8. Calcutta: Visva-Bharati Granthan Vibhaga, 1385 (B.S.), p. 471.
30. Tagore, Rabindranath. *Katha O Kahini.* Calcutta: Visva-Bharati Granthan Vibhaga, 1401 (B.S.), 169 p.
31. Tagore, Rabindranath. *Kshanika.* Visva-Bharati Granthan Vibhaga, 1359 (B.S.), p. 25.
32. Tagore, Rabindranath. *Sisu.* Calcutta: Visva-Bharati Granthan Vibhaga, 1958, p. 86.
33. Tagore, Rabindranath. *Chokher Bali.* Calcutta: Visva-Bharati Granthan Vibhaga, 1395 (B.S.), 242 p.
34. Tagore, Rabindranath. *Sesher Kavita.* Visva-Bharati Granthan Vibhaga, 1351 (B.S.), p. 44.

35. Tagore, Rabindranath. *Chhinapatravali*. Calcutta: Visva-Bharati Granthan Vibhaga, 1367 (B.S.), pp. 186-87.
36. Tagore, Rabindranath. *Kshanika*. Calcutta: Visva-Bharati Granthan Vibhaga, 1306 (B.S.), p. 5.
37. Tagore, Rabindranath. *Santiniketan Brahmacharyasram*. Santiniketan: Visva-Bharati, 1338 (B.S.), pp. 40-41.
38. Tagore, Rabindranath. *Katha Sahitya*. Calcutta: Visva-Bharati Granthan Vibhaga, 1367 (B.S.), p. 267.
39. Devarajan, G. *Research in library and information science*. New Delhi: Ess Publication, 2002, pp. 6-7.
40. Tagore, Rabindranath. *Rabindra Rachanavali*. Calcutta: Visva-Bharati Granthan Vibhaga, 1962.
41. Fairthorne, R.A. Empirical hyperbolic distribution (Bradford Ziff-Model bort) for bibliometric description and production. *Journal of Documentation*. 25, 1969; p. 326.
42. Chunkapura, Jose. *The God of Rabindranath Tagore*. Calcutta: Visva-Bharati Granthan Vibhaga, 2002, p. 87.
43. Tagore, Rabindranath. *Letters from Russia*. Calcutta: Visva-Bharati Granthan Vibhaga, 1367 (B.S.), pp. 9-11.
44. Tagore's comment on Granthagar to Kumar Munindra Debray. 1344. Later Kumar handed over the letter to Tagore. Kept in Rabindra Bhavana.
45. Tagore, Rabindranath. Santiniketan Adiparba. *Visva-Bharati Patrika*; 1349 (B.S.).
46. Mukhopadhyaya, Prabhatkumar. *Rabindrajivani O rabindrasahitya Prabeshak*. Vol. 3, Calcutta: Visva Bharati Granthan Vibhaga, 1359 (B.S.), p. 171.
47. *Visva-Bharati Annual Report 1921-22*.
48. Tagore, Rabindranath. *Siksha*. Santiniketan: Visva-Bharati,1342 (B.S.), Santiniketan; p. 270.
49. Tagore, Rabindranath. Sikshar Svangikaran. In *Siksha*. Vol. 1. Santiniketan: Visva-Bharati, 1351 (B.S.), p. 315.
50. *Visva-Bharati Bulletin no. 11*. Santiniketan: Visva-Bharati,1928, p. 1.
51. O'Connell, Kathleen M. *Rabindranath Tagore: the poet as educator*. Santiniketan: Visva-Bharati, 2002, p. 15.
52. Tagore, Rabindranath. *Rabindra Rachanavali*. Calcutta: Visva-Bharati Granthan Vibhaga, 1961, p. 582.
53. Tagore, Rabindranath. Schoolmaster. *Modern Review*. 36, 3; p. 313.
54. Tagore, Rabindranath. *Siksha*. Calcutta: Visva-Bharati Granthan Vibhaga, 1972, p. 20.
55. Tagore, Rabindranath. *Librarir Mukhyo Kartabya. Indian Library Journal*, Vol. 2, 3 and 4, 1929
56. Tagore, Rabindranath. *Personality*. London: Macmillan, 1959, p. 31.

57. Tagore, Rabindranath. *Rabindra Rachanavali*. Vol. 1. Calcutta: Visva-Bharati Granthan Vibhaga, 1961, p. 582.
58. Tagore, Rabindranath. *Siksha*. Calcutta: Visva-Bharati Granthan Vibhaga, 1972, p. 20.
59. Tagore, Rabindranath. *Personality*. London: Macmillan,1959, p. 116.
60. Yogeswar, R. *S.R. Ranganathan-pragmatic philosopher of information science: A personal biography*. Mumbai: Bharatiya Vidya Bhavan, 2001, p. 63.
61. Ray, Annadasankar. *Rabindranath: An artist in life*. In *Rabindranath Tagore centenary volume: 1861-1961*. New Delhi: Sahitya Akademi,1961, p. 217.
62. Ray, Niharranjan. *Rabindranath Tagore and Indian tradition*. In *Rabindranath Tagore centenary volume: 1861-1961*. New Delhi: Sahitya Academy, 1961, p. 223-232.
63. Thompson, Edward. *Rabindranath Tagore: Poet and Dramatist*. Calcutta: Rddhi India, 1979, p. 335.

Four

Role of Public Library in Tagore's Model of Rural Reconstruction: A Study

Introduction

Rabindranath Tagore (1861-1941) is known to the world for his extraordinary quality and versatility as a poet and writer. But he moved beyond literature and made outstanding contributions as an educationist, social reformer and religious thinker. The writings of Tagore were universal in expression and temper but rooted in oriental culture. His writings on literature, music, art, education, co-operative ideas, knowledge and its communication, etc. in one hand, on the other hand his activities on experimental school at Santiniketan (Abode of Peace), rural reconstruction programme at Sriniketan (Abode of Sri Lakshmi) all turned into gold with passage of time. This is true in case of Tagore's vision in his writings as well as its implementation at Santiniketan and Sriniketan.

Rabindranath acquired first hand experience of rural life in around December 1880 when he was looking after family estate at Silaidaha and Patisar (now in Bangladesh). Tagore narrated his experience as the "people used to come with their joys and sorrows, their claims and complaints. All these enabled me to form a true picture of villages. The outward appearance with rivers and wide plains, rice fields and huts nestling in the shelter of trees became familiar to me as also the inner story of rural life. The sufferings of the people became more and more intertwined with my daily work". He continues "gradually the sorrow and poverty of the villages became clear to me, and I began to grow restless to do something about it"[1]. The ideas took concrete shape with the establishment of rural development project at Sriniketan in November 1921. The central ideal of the Sriniketan was stated by Tagore as "The object of Srinketan is to bring back life in its completeness into the villages making them self-reliant and self-respectful, acquainted with the cultural tradition of their own country, and competent to make an efficient use of the modern resources for the improvement of their physical, intellectual and economic condition"[2] The underlying principle was to "… liberate these few villages in every respect so that all may receive education, a breeze of joy may blow once again, songs and music, recitation from epics and scriptures may fill them, as of yore."[3]. Main objective of this rural reconstruction programme according to its creator was "to try to flood the choked bed of village life with the stream of happiness."[4]. The aims and objects of the Institute, as originally set forth in details are:

1. "To win the friendship and affection of the villagers and cultivators by taking a real interest in all that concerns their life and welfare, and by making a lively effort to assist them in solving their most pressing problems;
2. To take the problems of the village and the field to the classroom for study, discussion and experiment in the farm,
3. To carry the knowledge and experience gained in the classroom and farm to the village and thereby to help the villagers ib their moral and material progress,
4. To work out an all-round system of elementary education in the villages with the ultimate object of developing ideas of citizenship…."[5]

To fulfill the objectives many faceted rural development programmes such as economic, village education, health, village organization, research and training, information communication in the form of feeder library, mobile library, village fair, recreation and celebration of festivals also took a pivotal place.

Mobile Library Service "Chalantika"

The public library service concept was developed and initiated with the very inception of Sriniketan Experiment of Rural Reconstruction. Tagore believed that "for the fundamental purpose of education is not merely to enrich ourselves through the fullness of knowledge, but also to establish the bond of love and friendship between man and man"[6]. For that he suggests "the highest educational institutions should assimilate knowledge from all sources and disseminate it for the benefit of the masses in order to strengthen their own foundation"[7]. Whenever, the occasion arose, Tagore always stressed the danger of inexpert service and the need to learn in order to serve. One can found in articles like *Tathya-Samgrah* (1919) how he recommended direct collection of data from the actual field of rural life. Consequently, surveys and researches on the problems of rural economy had been undertaken by the Institute.

But the information or knowledge so gained has to be disseminated to the masses. For dissemination of knowledge public library services in the form of mobile library services named "*Chalantika*" started in the year 1925 with initial collection of 200 books. The following table indicates the growth of collection and augmentation of its use by the rural masses in the initial years of its establishment.

Table 4.1: Collection Development and its Use: 1929-1934

Year	*No. of books*	*No. of books issued*
1929	450	729
1930	390	709
1931	400	600
1932	461	950
1933	512	1474
1934	1087	2457

Source: *Visva-Bharati Annual Report: 1929-34.*

In the year 1925, 1937 and 1940 the number of books of *Chalantika* was 200, 1200 and 1504 respectively. In the year 1939, the number of books issued were 2793[8]. At the initial stage there were only two mobile library branches at Bolpur and Goalpara in Birbhum district. The collection was mainly on fiction, biography, epigraphy, agriculture, health and children books. Pamphlets on agricultural problems, health care, primary education and rural reconstruction were published by the institute and circulated through mobile library. To make the rural people aware about the universe of knowledge a fortnight journal entitled "*Dese-Videse*" was published by the institute. For attracting people towards library, regular lecturer on various local problems and magic lantern-show were organized. In the year 1929, twenty-six lectures were delivered in nineteen villages, with a total attendance of 6,000 people[9]. Tagore believed "knowledge associated with joy and satisfaction increases power of learning, consequently our power of reception, apprehension, thinking and judgment develop easily and naturally[10].

Present Public Library Service

With the passage of time Rural Extension Centre (REC), Sriniketan took new approach in providing library services to the rural masses. The centre established rural libraries to strengthen the programme as well as to extend the services, as a centre of learning and store house of recorded knowledge, in collaboration with Raja Rammohun Roy Library Foundation (RRRLF) under the Ministry of Culture, Government of India, in the year 1975. Presently, there are 37 seven libraries scattered in 39 villages of 8 Gram Panchayats of two community development blocks namely Bolpur-Sriniketan and Illambazar of Birbhum district of West Bengal. Establishment of the libraries can be shown from the Table 4.2.

The basic objectives of establishment of these libraries are: development of knowledge power and dissemination of information; promotion and retention of acquired literacy skills; development of reading habits among the rural people; nurturing the cultural instinct by enriching the indigenous culture; open up a platform for sharing ideas and views with others and development of logical thinking and positive attitude of the villagers. To fulfill these objectives rural libraries are functioning as centre of information

Table 4.2: Establishment of Rural Libraries

Year	*Number of libraries established*
1975	9
1977	2
1980	4
1983	3
1986	4
1987	1
1991	6
1994	4
1999	2
2002	1
2005	1
2010	1
2012	1

Source: Annual Report of REC 2011-12.

dissemination, mass education, cultural exchange, literacy campaign, discussion, public relation and reader's amenity centre.

With the financial assistance of Rural Extension Centre (REC) and Visva-Bharati the rural libraries used to procure a good number of books every year. Regarding book selection the central committee for rural library services under (Rural Extension Centre) REC considers the opinion of the librarians, reader's requirements and also the recommendation of the library sub-committees constituted for every library. The libraries are providing services with the help of volunteer Librarians and Assistant Librarians under the local management of library sub committee. REC co-ordinates and gives necessary guidelines to the library sub- committees. Due to proper financial support as well as participatory management the collection of the libraries are growing as indicated in the Table 4.3.

Table 4.3: Growth of Collection

Year	*No. of books*	*No of books added during the year*
2006-07	85739	4,434
2007-08	91865	6,126
2008-09	97274	5,409
2009-10	1,02,356	5,082
2010-11	1,06,606	4,250

Source: *Annual report of* REC 2010-11.

For proper maintenance of the collection there is provision of regular binding of books. During last five years 2003-04 to 2010-11 total 3700 books were binded. One of the important features of the rural libraries is to collect books as donation from the rural people on 20th December Librarian Day every year. This helps to increase mass involvement and awareness of the people about library services. During 2009-2010 to 2011-12, 1103 number of books were collected. The numbers of users of the libraries are indicated by the following table.

Table 4.4: Enhancement/Decrease of Number of Readers

Year	*Male*	*Female*	*Total*
2006-07	2067	1024	3091
2007-08	1387	1022	2409
2008-09	1520	1212	2732
2009-10	1560	1280	2840
2010-2011	970	700	1671

The books used in the public libraries are mainly novel (17.22% of total books issued) but other categories of books on religion, travel and tourism, autobiography, etc. are also of demand. In the year 2007-08 total numbers of books on different subjects issued were 27700 as indicated in Table 4.5:

Table 4.5: Number of Books Issued During 2009-2010

Categories	*Number*
Novel	5241
Religious	2514
Travel and Tourism	2156
School Books	5214
Autobiography	2254
Children	5325
Bengali Fiction	945
Short Story	2675
Neo Literate	326
Vocational	1254
Other	2478
Total	**32540**

Table 4.6: Enhancement/Decrease of Use of Books During Last Five Years

Year	*Use of books*
2007-08	27700
2008-09	28356
2009-10	32540
2010-11	26970
2011-12	26784

The Librarians and Assistant Librarians run the rural libraries as volunteer under Rural Extension Centre (REC). In every month they attend the monthly seminars organized by REC. This seminar provides a platform, where the librarians can exchange the views about the functioning of the libraries. The educational status, occupations and caste composition of the volunteer Libraries are indicated by the following Table 4.7:

Table 4.7: Educational Qualification of Librarians/Assistant Librarians

Education	*No. of Librarians*
VII Standard	4
Madhyamik	13
Higher Secondary	14
Under Graduate	34
Post Graduate	2
Research Scholar	1
Total	**68**

Table 4.8: Occupation of the Volunteer Librarians

Occupation	*No. of Librarians*
Student	38
Service	7
Cultivation	16
Cultivation	7
Total	**68**

Table 4.9: Caste Composition of Librarians

Caste	*Frequency*
SC	17
ST	0
GEN	43
OBC	8

Raja Rammohun Roy Library Foundation (RRRLF) provides matching grant to Visva-Bharati for maintenance as well as augmentation of library resources. The fund is mainly used for procurement of books and equipments. The provision of funds for the rural libraries in the last five years is indicated below:

Table 4.10: Provision of Funds

Year	*RRRLF*	*Visva-Bharati*	*Total*
2007-08	2,50,000	2,50,000	5,00,000
2008-09	2,75,000	2,75,000	5,50,000
2009-10	3,50,000	3,50,000	7,00,000
2010-11	3,50,000	3,50,000	7,00,000
2011-2012	5,00,000	5,00,000	10,00,000

Besides the above grant RRRFL regularly sanction grant for conducting workshop/seminar on rural libraries. From the financial year 2003-04 RRRLF is regularly providing funds for constructing of library building. As a result in the current financial year 2011-12, new library building at Raipur and Srichandrapur Chandroy has been completed. The construction of new library building in Laldaha Saraswati Club and Khoskadampur Palli Seva Sangha are in the verge of completion. The ambitious project of providing computers with internet connectivity started. As a result, Raipur Yubo Sangha Pathagar three computers with internet and LAN connectivity.

Discussion

It is evident from the above figures that the number of readers (Table 4.4) is decreasing in rural libraries. The probable reasons as discussed with the librarians and users may be: vigorous inducement of electronic media, preoccupation and not to find time for libraries, timing of library hours, overall deterioration of reading habit, paucity of volunteers to facilitate library services. It can be observed from Table 4.7 that qualification of almost 50 per cent volunteer librarians are bellow graduation level. Even librarians having VIII standard qualification are providing library services, though they have came from different profession having different caste background. Although to run library services smoothly, as well as to popularize the library programme among the community REC, Visva-Bharati organizes regular discussion, meeting, exhibition, competition among readers, library visit, book collection from the villagers etc. For example in the year 2011-12 Library Day on 20th December observed in libraries, Wall Magazine published in 19 libraries, 50 cultural programmes were organized in 21 libraries, 34 discussion with readers took place[11].

It was observed during survey that there is scope for proper training of librarian to increase their efficiency for preparing catalogue, stock verification, development of network among libraries by sharing of resources and more emphasis on collection development in text books and books related to solve day to day problem in agriculture, cottage industry, animal husbandry as well as competitive examination. There is scope for upgrading these libraries as community information centre. For this REC have to be the nodal centre with educational, professional, agricultural, industrial etc. all kinds of information and these to be disseminate through rural libraries. Even to cope with the need of the hour Public Information Kiosk (PIK) can be established.

Conclusion

In the history of rural development in India, Rabindranath is known as a pioneer for his Sriniketan experiment on rural reconstruction. According to Tagore "it should be our mission to restore the full circulation of life's blood into these martyred limbs of society; to bring to the villagers health and knowledge; a wealth of space in which to live, a wealth of time in which to work, to rest and enjoy mutual respect which will give them dignity…"[12]. For this all the problems of rural development such as health, economy, education etc. were attacked at a time in Sriniketan experiment as they are interlinked with each other. For development of education besides formal education Tagore established night school, *Siksha-Satra* (school for rural people) with provision for vocational courses and

Lok Siksha Samsad (distance education programme) and mobile library "*Chanlantika*" for dissemination of information. The technique of 'expository method' of education followed by the social workers of Sriniketan was "reading books' for the villagers, who were illiterate or semiliterate[13]. In the year 1936-37 "there were 14 adult Santals who regularly read books from circulating library at Sriniketan. These books are circulated through the teacher, who lives in the villages. 42 books were issued altogether during this year amongst the Santals"[14].

Rabindranath was pioneer is providing mobile library service in India with the establishment of "*Chalantika*" in the year 1925. Dr. Ranganathan also provided mobile library service in Tanjore district of Madras Province with the help of bullock cart, later on he named it '*Librachine*'. In this connection we may quote biography of Ranganathan written by his son R. Yogeswar "MALA (Madras Library Association) had put up a stall at the Park Fair Exhibition of December 1930 at Madras. One exhibit was the idea of a traveling library to serve villages. Under Ranganathan's guidance, an artist had painted a picture of a bullock cart loaded with books and magazines. The general public had probably gone past this painting with little interest. But one visitor had made this exhibit worthwhile. It was a sub-engineer in government service one Kanakasabhai Pillai. It was not the potential of a travelling library to educate rural masses that had attracted his attention. The engineer in him had found the design of the cart very amateur. ....Pillai offered not only to design an appropriate cart with two bullocks, but to finance a vehicle to serve the region around his home-town of Mannargudi, about 40km south-east of Tanjore"[15].

Tagore's writings on library and establishment of library system at Santiniketan and Sriniketan are based on his educational philosophy of freedom of mind, freedom of heart and freedom of will. According Tagore the objective of education is "to give man unity of truth" and "the full realization of all the ideals in life through work and wisdom"[16]. His idea of library was alike with his idea of rural development "reform of education and regeneration of villages are the major task of my life"[17]. Tagore gave stress on rural library services to establish "a natural bond between education in the schools and colleges and the country outside them..."[18]. This is necessary to fulfill the objectives of education, as "the highest education is that which does not give us information but makes our life in harmony with all existence"[19]. For this library as knowledge centre has a good role to play. But to ensure fullest use of its resources, Tagore suggests "it is necessary that its contents should clearly and specially brought to notice" of reader with human touch, because "the library by itself imposes a responsibility—the responsibility relating to riches. Insofar as the library contains books, it attains fulfillment only through having those books read. It will not remain inactive; may it play an active role by issuing a call. Because ***tannashtam yannadiyate***"[20].

Notes and References

1. Extracts taken from the talk delivered by the poet to Sriniketan workers in summer 1939, later translated into English by Marjorie Sykes and first published in *Modern Review*, Nov. 1941.
2. Visva-Bharati Bulletin, No. 11, 1928, p. 12.
3. Tagore, Rabindranath. Sriniketan address. *Modern Review*. November 1941.
4. Tagore, Rabindranath. *City and Village*. Calcutta: Visva-Bharati Granthan Vibhaga, 1976, p. 24.
5. Visva-Bharati Bulletin No. 6. Santiniketan: Visva-Bharati, 1921.
6. Tagore, Rabindranath. *Siksha*. Calcutta: Visva-Bharati Granthan Vibhaga, 1342 (B.S.), p. 270.
7. Tagore, Rabindranath. *Sikshar Svangikaran*. In *Siksha*. Calcutta: Visva-Bharati Granthan Vibhaga, 1351 (B.S.), p. 315.
8. Chakraborty, Satyadas. *Sriniketaner gorar katha*. Srinikatan: Sahitya Samaj, 1985, pp. 51-52.
9. Lal, Prem Chand. *Reconstruction and education in rural India*. London: George Allen & Unwin, 1952, pp. 82-83.
10. Tagore, Rabindranath. *Siksha*. Calcutta: Visva-Bharati Granthan Vibhaga, 1973, p. 226. Tr. by the author.
11. *Rural Extension Centre, Visva-Bharati Annual Report 2010-11*. Sriniketan: Visva-Bharati, 2011.

12. Elmhirst, Leonard K. *Poet and plowman*. Calcutta: Visva-Bharati Granthan Vibhaga, 1975, p. 39. Introduction of the essay The Robbery of the Soil written by Rabindranath.
13. *Visva-Bharati Annual Report and Audited Accounts* 1933-34. Santiniketan: Visva-Bharati, 1934, p. 29.
14. *Visva-Bharati Annual Report and Audited Accounts*. 1936-37. Santiniketan: Visva-Bharati, 1937, p. 28.
15. Yogeswar, R.S.R. *Ranganathan-pragmatic Philosopher of Information Science: A Personal Biography*. Mumbai: Bharatiya Vidya Bhavan, 2001, p. 63.
16. Tagore, Rabindranath. *Personality*. London: Macmillan, 1959, p. 31.
17. Tagore, Rabindranath. *Rabindra Rachanavali*. Vol. 1. Calcutta: Visva-Bharati Granthan Vibhaga, 1961, p. 582.
18. Tagore, Rabindranath. *Siksha*. Calcutta: Visva-Bharati Granthan Vibhaga, 1972, p. 20.
19. Tagore, Rabindranath. *Personality*. London: Macmillan, 1959, p. 116.
20. Tagore, Rabindranath. *Librarir Mukhyo Kartabya*. Tagore as Chairman of Reception Committee of All India Library Association prepared this speech in Dec 1928. Hiremdranath Dutta read out this paper in his absence due to illness. It appears in *Indian Library Journal*, Vol. 2, 3 and 4, 1929.

SECTION-II

Bibliometric Study of Select Writings of Tagore

Five

Songs of Rabindranath Tagore: A Bibliometric Study

Introduction

Rabindranath Tagore, a renaissance figure, colossal in vigour, volume and variety, put forward Indian literature to the world. Essentially known as a poet, but he was a dramatist, writer of short stories, novelist, philosopher, composer and singer, innovator in education and rural development, actor, director, painter, cultural ambassador and what not. Rabindranath, the writer of two National anthems, has composed more than two thousand songs known as Rabindra Sangit that have become a symbol of cultural ethos of both India and Bangladesh.

Rabindranath composed his first poem at the age of eight and by the end of his life, he has written twenty-five volumes of poetry, fifteen plays, ninety-five short stories, eleven novels, thirteen volumes of essays; initiated and edited various journals; prepared Bengali textbooks, penned thousands of letters; and crossing the age of seventy created more than two thousand paintings. All these writings and paintings come under the purview of Tagoreana. It starts with the publication of first poem signed in his own name *Hindu Melār Upahār* (The Gift of Hindu Mela) in the bilingual *Amrita Bazar Patrika* (25th February, 1875). The poet read this poem at 9th annual conference of Hindumela on 12th February,

1875. The poem was of 22 stanzas with 88 lines. It was published in the *Prabāshi Patrikā* in 1338 (B.S.) Magh issue[1] and first verse narrative *Banaphul* (The Wild Flower) published in *Jnanānkur* and *Pratibimbha*. The last birth day (7th May 1941) of his life is marked with the publication of three books, *Janmadine* in verse (On my birthday), *Galpa-salpa*, a collection of short stories, My *boyhood days*, the English version of *Chhelebelā*.

Tagore's long literary career has been classified by different scholars from different viewpoints of literary development. Chunkapura classified it as youth and early adulthood writings (1878-1900), *Gitānjali* period (1900-1912), the year of matured reflections (1912-1927) and the final years (1927-1941)[2]. Thompson classified development of Tagoreana as early life and poetry (1861-1886), The *Śileida* and *Sādhanā* period (1887-1897), unrest and change (1898-1905), *Gitānjali* period (1905-1919) and finally internationalism (1919-1941)[3]. Majumdar leaving aside the period of radiant dawn 1875-1880, before the rise of the effulgent sun, divided the literary life of the poet into four epochs. The first period covers seventeen years from 1881-1897, from the date of writing of *Bau Thakurānir Hāt* to that of composing the *Lakshmir Parikshā*. The second period is that of full maturity extending from 1898 to 1913. The next thirteen years of third period from 1914 to 1926 may be called the age of rejuvenation of the poet and his revolt against the conventional society. The last period covering fifteen years, 1927 to 1941 is the age of glorious and picturesque sunset[4]. Tagore's biographer Prabhatkumar though not categorically distinguished writings of Tagore like others but pointed out different phases of life as littérateur in the making, the flower blossoms, the humanitarian takes his stand; the nationalist takes shape, the brotherhood of man, the diffusion of culture[5]. Kripalani pointed out different phases as adolescence, youth, maturity, a man among men, a world citizen, world in one nest, old world and new, between two worlds[6]. It is obvious that growth of Tagoreana with the passage of time reflected faithfully the diverse tendencies of his age. But at the same time these help to usher in a new epoch in Indian history.

Objectives

The study has the following major objectives:

- To find out the growth pattern of Rabindra Sangit.
- To trace the trend of publication of Rabindra Sangit.
- To make quantitative assessment of Tagore's writings on songs in different literary forms.
- To make an assessment of Sangit in Tagoreana in respect of different phases of Tagore's literary career, and
- Try to find out whether there is any impact of personal sorrow on composing songs.

Methodology and Source

As research methodology, bibliometric technique is used, as an attempt "to analyse quantitatively the properties and behaviour of recorded knowledge"[7]. In this study statistical bibliometric technique is followed as it helps to "... shed light on the process of written communication and of the nature and course of development of discipline by means of counting and analyzing the various facets of written communication"[8].

As the source book *Gitabitan*[9] (Book of notation), *Rabindra Rachanāvali* (Collected works of Tagore)[10] and *Sangitchintā* (Thoughts on music)[11] were consulted for this study. Besides, primary and secondary sources in the form of original works or first editions of Tagore's work kept in Rabindra Bhavan[12] were consulted. Moreover, a wide range of secondary sources in the form of books and articles both in Bengali and English were consulted to corroborate and critically evaluate for the purpose of interpretation.

Rabindra Sangit: Its Growth and Publication

Tagore's first collection of songs *Rabichchāya* was published in 1292 (B.S.). It has been stated in the introduction of the book that "this volume includes almost all the songs composed by Rabindrababu up to the last date of the year 1291[BS]"[13]. Later on, in the year

1300 (B.S.) the book on songs entitled *Gāner Bahi o Vālmiki Pratibhā* was published including songs of the dance drama *Vālmiki Pratibhā*[14]. In the year 1303 (B.S.) Tagore's first *Kabya Granthāvali* was published which included songs of *Gān* (Song) and *Brahmasangit*. Under the editorship of Mohit Chandra Sen, collected works of Rabindranath was published organizing the same on the basis of the theme. *Gān* was included in volume 8 in the year 1310 (B.S.)[15].

Later on *Gān* was published by Jogendranath Sarkar of City Book Society in the year 1315 (B.S.). There were 528 songs in this book. In the next year (1909) second edition of *Gān* was published by Indian Publishing House. This edition tried to collect and publish all the songs of Rabindranath which numbered 727. It was declared in the introduction of *Gān* published in 1316 (B.S.) that "this book published all the best songs of Poet starting from his boyhood days up to date but failed to achieve complete success"[16]. The publisher had to give this statement because at the beginning of first decades of twentieth century research on Tagoreana was not started on scientific basis. This edition organized the songs on the basis of theme or subject such as season, nature, etc.

Indian Publishing House, Calcutta published collected works of Rabindranath Tagore in the year 1915-16. *Gān* finds its place in tenth volume[17]. But it was again an incomplete effort. Besides that individual volume was not available for sale. After the establishment of Santiniketan Press in the year 1323 (B.S) publication of *Rabindrasangit* started with notation such as *Gitapanchāsika* (Asvin,1325 BS), *Baitālik* (Chaitra, 1325 BS), *Gitabithikā* (Baishakh, 1326 BS), *Ketaki* (Shravan, 1326 BS), *Śefāli* (Bhādra, 1326 BS), *Kābyagiti* (Poush, 1326 BS), etc.[18]

In the year 1338 (BS) on the occasion of the celebration of seventieth year of the Poet, a collection of Rabindrasangit was published under the title *Gitabitān*. The first and second volumes were published in Āsvin of 1338 (BS) and the third volume in Śrāvan of 1339 (B.S). The volumes were published by Jagadananda Ray, a teacher of Santiniketan from Visva-Bharati Granthalaya, 210 Cornwallis Street, Calcutta. The editorial responsibility for this publication was vested on Sudhirchandra Kar. Professor

Amiyachandra Chakraborty was adviser to the editor. In the first edition of *Gitabitān* the songs were organized on the basis of date of publication not on the themes. In the introduction Prof. Kar wrote "Volume two and three include 1128 songs from adolescent to songs of *Basanta* dance drama. 148 songs were not included as per the direction of the Poet"[19]. The first and second volumes of *Gitabitān* include songs of Rabindranath up to 1300 (B.S). The songs were organized on the basis of the themes as Tagore thought arrangement on the basis of themes only will be appropriate.

Year-wise distribution of the publication of books on songs would help to know the growth pattern of book on song written by Rabindranath (Table 5.1).

Rabindranath wrote many dance dramas where many songs exist. He has also specially written songs for particular dance dramas. All those songs are also included. In dance dramas *Nritya Nātya, Chitrāngadā, Chandālikā* and *Śyamā* there are 150 songs. Similarly, in the dance drama *Navin, Varshāmangal, Sāradotsav, Vasanta, Sundar* and *Phālguni* there are 126 songs. In the dance drama *Vālmiki Pratibhā, Kāl-Mrigayā, Māyār Khelā, Prakritir Pratisodh* there are 165 songs.

Rabindranath used songs in his dramas as well which may be observed from Table 5.2.

Totaling the number of songs given against the books cannot reveal the total number of songs written by Rabindranath as many songs were repeated in various books. Moreover, the number of songs increased in different editions of the same book. For example, the first edition (1881) of *Vālmiki Pratibhā* contains 27 songs but the number increased to 53 in the second edition (1886). The first and second volumes of *Gitabitān* containing 1500 songs was printed in Bhādra, 1346 (B.S) and published after his death. The third volume was published after the demise of Rabindranath in 1357 (B.S) by Visva-Bharati Granthan Vibhaga (publishing department of Visva-Bharati). According to the index of the new edition (Māgh, 1379 B.S) of third volume, the total number of songs is 732. Out of these songs in three volumes we find notation of 1890 songs in 60 volumes of *Swarabitan*. For example, *Bhānusimha Thākurer Padāvali*

Table 5.1: Books on Songs in Tagoreana

Age of the Poet	Title	Year of Publication	No. of Songs
19	*Vālmiki Pratibhā*	1881	27
20	*Bhagnahriday*	1881	11
20	*Rudrachandā*	1881	02
21	*Kāl-Mrigayā*	1882	39
23	*Bau-Thākurānir Hāt*	1884	11
23	*Prakritir Pratiśodh*	1884	10
23	*Nalini*	1884	04
23	*Śaiśav Sangit*	1884	11
23	*Bhānusimha Thākurer Padāvali*	1884	22
23	*Chhabi o Gān*	1884	02
24	*Rabichchhāya*	1885	201
25	*Kadi o Komal*	1886	11
25	*Vālmiki Pratibhā – 2nd Ed.*[20]	1886	53
26	*Rājarshi*	1887	02
27	*Mayār Khelā*	1888	63
28	*Rājā o Rāni*	1889	09
29	*Visarjan*	1890	06
29	*Mānasi*	1890	04
31	*Chitrāngadā*	1892	47
31	*Godāy Galad*	1892	01
32	*Gāner Bahi o Vālmiki Pratibhā*[21]	1893	423
33.	*Megh o Raudra*	1894	01
33	*Sonār Tari*	1894	03
35	*Chitrā*	1896	09
35	*Kābyagranthāvali*[22]	1896	480
39	*Kalpanā*	1900	16
39	*Kshanikā*	1900	04
39	*Naivedya*	1901	17
41	*Kabyagrantha*[23]	1903	428
43	*Rabindragranthāvali (Hitavādi Ed)*[24]	1904	421
44	*Bāul*	1905	20
45	*Kheyā*	1906	08
46	*Bini Paisār Bhoj*	1907	01
46	*Baśikaran*	1907	02
47	*Prajāpatir Nirbandha*	1908	25
47	*Gān*[25]	1908	528
47	*Śāradotsav*	1908	10
48	*Prāyaśchitta*[26]	1909	23
48	*Gān*	1909	727
48	*Śiśu*	1909	01
49	*Gitānjali*	1910	85
49	*Gitalipi—Vol. 1*	1910	18
49	*Gitalipi—Vol. 2*	1910	17
49	*Gitalipi—Vol. 3*	1910	15
49	*Rāja*	1910	25
50	*Gitalipi—Vol. 4*	1911	15
50	*Gitalipi—Vol. 5*	1911	16

(Contd.)

Table 5.1 (*Contd.*)

Age of the Poet	*Title*	*Year of Publication*	*No. of Songs*
51	*Achalāyatan*	1912	23
53	*Utsarga*	1914	01
53	*Gān*[27]	1914	395
53	*Dharmasangit*[28]	1914	325
53	*Giti-mālya*	1914	87
53	*Gitāli*	1914	66
54	*Kāvyagrantha—Vol. 10*[29]	1916	492
54	*Phālguni*	1916	30
55	*Ghare-Bāire*	1916	04
55	*Balāka*	1916	04
55	*Chaturanga*	1916	01
55	*Śesher Rātri*	1916	01
57	*Guru*	1918	07
57	*Gitalekha-Vol. 1*	1918	29
57	*Gitalipi—Vol. 6*	1918	13
57	*Gitapanchāśika*	1918	50
57	*Baitālik*	1918	36
58	*Gitalekhā —Vol. 2*	1919	28
58	*Gitabithikā*	1919	22
58	*Ketaki*	1919	31
58	*Śefāli*	1919	28
59.	*Kāvyagiti*	1920	23
59	*Arupratan*	1920	39
60	*Varshāmangal*	1921	17
60	*Gitalekha—Vol. 3*	1921	24
60	*Rinśodh*	1921	07
61	*Muktadhārā*	1922	14
61	*Varshāmangal*	1922	18
61	*Lipikā*	1922	01
61	*Nabagitikā—Vol. 1*	1922	34
61	*Nabagitikā—Vol. 2*	1922	59
62	*Vasanta*	1923	23
64	*Puravi*	1925	01
64	*Grihapraveś*	1925	09
64	*Pravāhini*	1925	235
65	*Chirakumār Sabhā*	1926	32
65	*Śodh-bodh*	1926	03
65	*Ritu-utsav*[30]	1926	108
65	*Natir Pujā*	1926	11
65	*Raktakarabi*	1926	08
65	*Gitamālikā—Vol. 1*	1926	52
66	*Rituranga*	1927	29
67	*Śesh Rakshā*	1928	09
68	*Paritrān*	1929	21
68	*Tapati*	1929	10
68	*Mahuā*	1929	12
69	*Gitamālika—Vol. 2*	1930	50

(*Contd.*)

Table 5.1 (*Contd.*)

Age of the Poet	Title	Year of Publication	No. of Songs
70	*Navin*	1931	21
70	*Sāpmochan*	1931	23
70	*Gitabitān—Vol. 1 and 2*	1931	1128
71	*Gitabitān—Vol. 3*	1932	357
71	*Gitotsav*	1932	03
71	*Pariśodh*	1932	30
72	*Tāser Des*	1933	22
73	*Śravangāntha*	1934	22
73	*Chār Adhyāy*	1934	01
74	*Vithikā*	1935	04
75	*Nritya-nātya Chitrangadā*	1936	47
75	*Arupratan*	1936	25
77	*Chandālika Nritya-nātya*	1938	51
77	*Muktir Upāy*	1938	02
78	*Śyamā*	1939	52
79	*Sānāi*	1940	23
80	*Badnām*	1941	01
80	*Śeshlekhā*	1941	02

Table 5.2: Songs in Dramas

SL. No.	Drama	No. of Songs
1.	*Rāja o Rāni*	09
2.	*Visarjan*	06
3.	*Godāy Galad*	01
4.	*Prayaśchitta*	23
5.	*Rājā*	25
6.	*Achalāyatan*	23
7.	*Guru*	07
8.	*Arupratan (1920 ed.)*	39
9.	*Rinśodh*	07
10.	*Muktadhāra*	14
11.	*Grihapraveś*	09
12.	*Chirakumār Sabhā*	32
13.	*Śodh-bodh*	03
14.	*Natir Pujā*	11
15.	*Raktakarabi*	08
16.	*Śesh Rakshā*	09
17.	*Paritrān*	21
18.	*Tapati*	10
19.	*Śāpmochan*	23
20.	*Pariśodh*	30
21.	*Tāser Des*	22
22.	*Arupratan (1936)*	25

contains 22 songs but we find notation of 10 songs only. Tagore provided notation to many lyric poems and included in *Gitabitân*.

Still there are many song-like poems of Tagore which requires notation[31].

Table 5.3 indicates that Rabindranath started writing songs in 1875 well before writing the verse *Kavi-Kahini* in 1878. It is also clear that Tagore wrote highest number of songs (N= 91) at the age of 23 in the year 1884-85 (1291 B.S.) and continued writing songs till his death. A literary analysis of songs would reveal that *Rabindrasangit* covers different aspects like *prem* (love), *puja* (prayer), *prakriti* (nature), and so on. The data in Table 5.3 is graphically presented in Fig. 5.1.

Table 5.3: Year-wise Growth of Rabindra Sangit

Year (Bangiya Śakabda within Brackets)	*Age of Rabindranath*	*Number of Songs*	*Cumulative Total*
1875 (1281)	13	1	1
1875 (1282)	14	1	2
1877-78 (1284)	16	9	11
1878 (1285)	17	10	21
1879-80 (1286)	18	16	37
1880-81 (1287)	19	45	82
1881-82 (1288)	20	32	114
1882-83 (1289)	21	47	161
1883-84 (1290)	22	56	217
1884-85 (1291)	23	91	308
1885-86 (1292)	24	45	353
1886-87 (1293)	25	47	400
1887-88 (1294)	26	19	419
1888-89 (1295-96)	27	60	479
1889-90 (1296-97)	28	11	490
1890 (1297)	29	6	496
1892 (1298)	30	2	498
1892-93 (1299)	31	13	511
1893-94 (1300)	32	27	538
1894-95 (1301)	33	9	547
1895-96 (1302-03)	34	33	580
1896-97 (1303-04)	35	23	603
1897-98 (1304)	36	30	633
1899 (1305)	37	6	639
1900 (1306)	38	24	663
1900-01 (1307)	39	50	713
1901-02 (1308)	40	13	726
1902-03 (1309)	41	14	740
1903-04 (1310)	42	5	745
1904-05 (1311)	43	10	755

(Contd.)

Table 5.3 *(Contd.)*

Year (Bangiya Śakabda within Brackets)	*Age of Rabindranath*	*Number of Songs*	*Cumulative Total*
1905-06 (1312)	44	37	792
1906-07	45	7	799
1907-08 (1314)	46	9	808
1908-09 (1315)	47	19	827
1909-10 (1316-17)	48	76	903
1910-11 (1317)	49	66	969
1911-12 (1318-19)	50	45	1014
1912 (1319)	51	2	1016
1913-14 (1320-21)	52	64	1080
1914-15 (1321-22)	53	114	1194
1915-16 (1322-23)	54	25	1219
1916-17 (1323-24)	55	1	1220
1917-18 (1324-25)	56	14	1234
1918-19 (1325-26)	57	33	1267
1919-20 (1326-27)	58	19	1286
1921-22 (1328-29)	60	57	1343
1922-23 (1329-30)	61	97	1440
1923-24 (1330-31)	62	31	1471
1924-25 (1331-32)	63	33	1504
1925-26 (1332-33)	64	99	1603
1926-27 (1333-34)	65	61	1664
1927-28 (1334-35)	66	46	1710
1928-29 (1335-36)	67	8	1718
1929-30 (1336-37)	68	38	1756
1930-31 (1337-38)	69	26	1782
1932-33 (1339-40)	71	8	1790
1933-34 (1340-41)	72	38	1828
1934-35 (1341-42)	73	10	1838
1935-36 (1342-43)	74	64	1902
1936-37 (1343-44)	75	49	1951
1937-38 (1344-45)	76	84	2039
1938-39 (1345-46)	77	84	2123
1939-40 (1345-46)	78	46	2169
1940 (1347)	79	7	2176
1941 (1348)	80	2	2178

Source: Gitabitan.

Tagore's Writings on Sangit: A Bibliometric Study

Rabindranath not only composed songs and gave tunes to it, but also wrote on different aspects of songs in different literary forms as indicated in the Table 5.4.

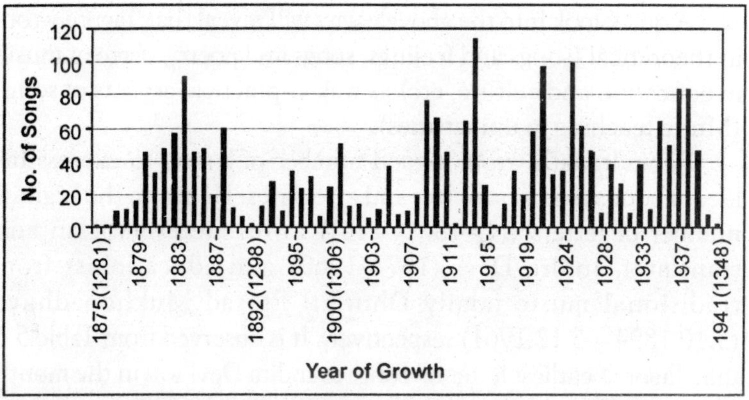

Fig. 5.1: Growth of Rabindra Sangit

Table 5.4: Writings on Sangit in Different Literary Forms

Essays	*Letters*	*Diary*	*Part of Essays*	*Add-ress*	*For-ward*	*Inter-view*	*Conver-sation*	*Auto-biogra-phy*	*Total*
18	51	20	18	4	1	1	3	2	118

It is clear from Table 5.4 that Rabindranath wrote on songs almost in all literary forms, though correspondence occupies a prominent place in it.

Table 5.5: Essays

Sl. No.	*Titles*	*First Published (B.S.)*
1.	*Sangit o Bhāb*	Bhārati, Jaishthya-Ashādh, 1288.
2.	*Sangit o Kabitā*	Bhā rati, Māgh,1288
3.	*Gān Sambandhe Prabandha*	Prabāsi, Baiśākh, 1319
4.	*Antar Bāhir*	Bhārati, Śrāvan, 1319
5.	*Sangit*	Bhārati, Agrahāyana, 1319
6.	*Sonār Kāthi*	Sabujpatra, Jaisthya,1322
7.	*Sangiter Mukti*	Sabujpatra, Bhādra, 1324
8.	*Āmader Sangit*	Sabujpatra, Bhādra, 1328
9.	*Śikshā o Samskritite Sangiter Sthān*	Prabāsi, Phālgun,1342
10.	*Kathā o Sur, Part 1*	Bichitrā, Agrahāyana, 1344
11.	*Kathā o Sur, Part 2*	Prabāsi, Ashādh, 1346
12.	*Alāp o Alochanā Part 1 and 2*	Bangabāni, Jaishthya,1332
13.	*Alāp o Alochanā Part 3*	Prabāsi, Kārtik, 1334
14.	*Alāp o Alochanā Part 4*	Bichitrā, Phālgun, 1344
15.	*Visvavidyālaye Sangit Śikshā*	Prābasi, Agrahāyana, 1335

A quick look into the above essays will reveal that Tagore wrote in theoretical (songs and feelings, songs and poetry, place of music in education and culture, etc) as well as practical aspects of songs (Music teaching in universities).

Rabindranath wrote a good number of letters to express his ideas about songs to scholars and associates. He wrote the highest number of letters (N=18, N=16)) to his niece-musician and translator, Indira Devi (1873-1960) and educationist from traditional music family Dhurjati Prasad Mukhopadhaya (5.10.1894—5.12.1961) respectively. It is observed from Table 5.6 that Tagore's earliest letter on songs to Indira Devi was in the month of June 1889 and latest to Sudharani Sen (29.3.1939).

Table 5.6: Letters

Sl. No.	*Name*	*No. of Letters*	*Date(s) of Writings*
1.	Dhurjati Prasad Mukhopadhaya	16	13.8.1931, 1 Bhādra (18.8.1931), 12 Bhādra (7.9.1931), 1932, 10 Māgh 1341 (24.1.1934), 16 Chaitra 1341 (30.3.1934), 7.1.1935, 21.3.1935, 9.4.1935, 15.5.1935, 16.5.1935, 6.7.1935, 29.4.1936, 8.10.1937
2.	Indira Devi	18	6.1889, 18.1.1891, 6.10.1891, 5.7.1892, 10.7.1892, 21.7.1892, 10.8.1894, 10.9.1894, 21, 11, 1894, 22.1.1895, 1.3.1895, 2.5.1895, 5.7.1895, 20.9.1895, 26.9.1895, 15.12.1895, 13.1.1935, 2.6.1936,
3.	Jyotirindranath Tagore	1	3.6.1914
4.	Priyanath Sen	1	1915
5.	Amiya Chakraborty	1	14.2.1939
6.	Nirmal Kumari Mahalanobis	3	8.8.1929, 8.8.1930, 11.12.1938
7.	Dilip Kumar Roy	6	18, 10, 1929, 10.11.1929, 29.7.1937, 29.10.1937, 6.2.1938.
8.	Pulinbehari Sen	1	20.11.1937
9.	Sudharani Sen	1	29.3.1939
10.	Sahana Devi	2	4.4.1938, 29, 4, 1938
11.	Janakinath Basu	1	20.12.1938

Table 5.7: Diary

Sl. No.	*Diary*	*No. of writings*	*Date(s) of Writings*
1.	Paschim Yātrir Dāyeri	6	7.10.1924,7.1.1925,11.2.1925,12.2.1925, 14.2.1925,15.2.1925
2.	Europe Yātrir Dāyeri	5	19.9.1890, 10.10.1890,16.10.1890 (2) 22.10.1890
3.	Japan-Yātri	1	29.5 1916-7.9.1916
4.	Java-Yatrir Patra	5	31.8.1927,7.9.1927,14.9.1927, 17.9.1927 10.9.1927
5.	Pārasya-Yātri	3	17.4.1932, 29.9.1932, 5.5.1932

During his travel to different countries Tagore used to write diary. In all such diaries one can find his concern and vision on songs as reflected in Table 5.7.

Table 5.8: Address

Sl. No.	*Date*	*Place*	*Occasion*
1.	17.3.1922	University Institute Hall, Calcutta	Prize Distribution Ceremony of Sangit Sangha
2.	1 Asvin 1331 (18.9.1924)	Presidency College, Calcutta	Address to the Students of Presidency College
3.	27.12.1934	Senate House, Calcutta	All Bengal Music Competition and Conference Inaugural address
4.	23.6.1940		Address in the inaugural function of a Rabindrasangit Teaching Centre "Gitāli"

Tagore's concern for music particularly its role as a medium of expression of feelings has amply been reflected in his addresses.

Table 5.9: Conversation

Sl. No.	*Place*	*Conversation with*
1.	Villeneuve,24.6.1926	Romain Rolland
2.	August, 1930	Albert Einstein
3.	Geneva, June 1930	H.G. Wells

One can find Tagore's opinion on music and musical instruments in his conversation with Rolland, Einstein and Wells.

For example, Tagore told Rolland "You know, I am not merely a writer of verse; I am keenly interested in music and I myself compose songs. I have always felt puzzled why there are such great differences in musical form in different countries. Surely music should be more universal than other forms of art, for its vehicle is easy to reproduce and transmit from one country to another"[32].

Rabindranath gave an interview to Marguerite Wilkinson where he expressed his opinion about music with these words "Sometimes I make the words first and then put music with them later. Sometimes, I make a melody first and then put words with it. Sometimes, the music is subordinated to the words. Sometimes, the words are subordinated to music"[33]. Two autobiographies of Tagore —*Jivansmriti*[34] and *Chhelebelā*[35] also indicate about his first music learning, music culture of the Tagore family, etc.

Conclusion

It is very difficult to count the total number of books in Tagoreana or to indicate year-wise literary output, as many of them were first published in the form of a booklet/address/pamphlet and later published as a book or included as a part of a book. This is particularly true in case of *Swaralipi* (books of notation known as *Swaravitan*) as many of them were also published as separate book like *Nrityanāātya Syamā* is *Swaravitan* 19. For that reason only individual *Swaravitān* is treated as a separate book while showing the growth of Tagoreana. Moreover, in the case of literature what matters is the depth of knowledge and wisdom expressed in writings not the numbers. The romantic touches reflected in the songs of Rabindranath come from his rapport with the beauty and mystery in nature deeply rooted in social, family and individual life. These reflections can never be measured in mere statistical figures. Even it becomes difficult to categorise his writings. For example, Rabindranath's poetry is so vast, varied and voluminous that it is very difficult to schematize. Before he was eighteen, he had published nearly seven thousand lines of verse[36]. One critic, historian Niharranjan Ray has tried to depict six-fold pattern of growth of Tagoreana: Germination and Early Blossoms (1872-88),

Fruits of Maturity (1888-1900), Fruits of Offerings (1901-1913), The Nest and the Sky (1914-25), New Flowers and Fruits (1926-37) and The Sunset Glow (1937-41). But the metaphor breaks down at least in two occasions. When the same critic tells us that in *Sāndhya Sangit* (Evening Songs, 1882) Tagore had come of age it is difficult not to disagree. He admits no grand generalization will hold, no poet is mature at twenty-one[37]. Thus, it may be concluded that Rabindranath composed music throughout his literary career (1875-1941). He started composing music in 1875, even three years before the publication of his verse narrative *Kavi-Kāhini* in 1878. Regarding his song Rabindranath himself felt "I get lost in my songs, and then I think that these are my best works; I get quite intoxicated. I often feel that, if all my poetry is forgotten, my songs will live with my countrymen, and have a permanent place"[38].

Rabindranath faced a good number of deaths in his life time such as mother Sarada Devi (10.3.1875); bauthan [wife of Jyotirindranath] Kadambini Devi (19.4.1884); elder brother Hemendranath Tagore (5.6.1984); nephew Balendranath (22.8.1899); wife Mrinalini Devi (23.11.1902); second daughter Renuka (19.9.1903): associate of Santiniketan Satischandra Ray (1.2.1904); father Debendranath Tagore (9.1.1905); son Samindranath (Nov, 1907); daughter Madhurilata (13.5.1918); elder sister Saratkumari (11.4.1920); elder brother Satyendranath (9.1.1923); close associate at Santiniketan Pearson (24.9.1923); elder brother Jyotirindranath (4.3.1925); elder brother Dwijendranath (18.1.1926); grand daughter Nitindranath (29.7.1932); Santiniketan associates C.F. Andrews (5.4.1940), nephew Surendranath (3.5.1940), to name only a few[39]. If we consider the rise of *Sun* with the first composition of song (1875) or writing *Kavi-Kāhini* in the year 1878 and *Sunset* (demise of Rabindranath) in 1941, then it can be concluded that the untold sorrow inflicted by the death of family members or close associates could not stop his mighty pen. The poet's son Rathindranath wrote in this respect "vicissitudes of life, pain and afflictions never upset the equanimity of my father's mind. His inward peace was not disturbed by any calamity, however painful. Some inner resources gave him the power to face and rise above misfortunes of the most painful nature"[40]. Tagore himself wished "May the joy and sorrows, hopes and desires of our country be immortalized in the Elysian fields of song"[41]. Thus, to conclude, to believe him, his life and works form a parable of the play of the Finite and Infinite (*Seemā-Aseemer Pālā*). It is impossible to judge to which he was more loyal — to the sky or the nest, the wings or the roots?

Notes and References

1. Bandyopadhaya, B. *Rabindra grantha-parichay (1878-1943).* Calcutta: Sahitya-Niketan, 1349 (B.S.), p. 28.
2. Chunkapura, J. *The God of Rabindranath Tagore: A study of the Evolution of his understanding of God.* Calcutta: Visva-Bharati Granthan Vibhaga, 2002, p. 351.
3. Thompson, E. *Rabindranath Tagore: Poet and dramatist.* Calcutta: Rddhi-India, 1979, p. 335.
4. Majumdar, B. *Heroines of Tagore: a study in the transformation of Indian society 1875-1941.* Calcutta: Firma K.L. Mukhopadhyay, 1968, p. 15.
5. Mukhopadhaya, Prabhatkumar. *Life of Tagore*. New Delhi: Indian Book Company, 1975, p. 208. Tr. from Bengali by Sisirkumar Ghosh.
6. Kripalani, K. *Rabindranath Tagore: A biography*. Calcutta: Visva-Bharati Granthan Vibhaga, 1980, p. 491.
7. Pritchard, A. Statistical bibliography or bibliometrics. *Journal of Documentation.* 24 ((4)(1969) 348.
8. Hulme, E.W. *Statistical bibliography in relation to the growth of modern civilization.* London: Grafton, 1923, p. 44.
9. Tagore, Rabindranath. *Gitabitan—3 Vols.* Calcutta: Visva-Bharati Granthan Vibhaga, 1338 (B.S.), p. 864.
10. Tagore, Rabindranath. *Rabindra Rachanavali—17 Vols.* Calcutta: Visva-Bharati Granthan Vibhaga, 1365 (B.S.)
11. Tagore, Rabindranath. *Sangitchinta.* Calcutta: Visva-Bharati Granthan Vibhaga, 1399 (B.S.), p. 368.
12. Rabindra Bhavan is the Tagore Research Centre built in the centenary year 1961 of Rabindranath at Santiniketan.
13. Tagore, Rabindranath. *Rabichāchhāyā.* Calcutta: Jogendranarayan Mitra, 1292 (B.S.), p. 1.
14. Tagore, Rabindranath. *Gāner bahi o Vālmiki Pratibhā.* Calcutta: Adi Brahma Samaj, 1330 (B.S.), p. 407.

15. Tagore, Rabindranath. *Kāvya-grantha. Vol. 8*. Calcutta: Majumder Library, p. 338.
16. Tagore, Rabindranath. *Gān*. Allahabad: Indian Press, 1316 (B.S.), p. 412.
17. Tagore, Rabindranath. *Gān*. Calcutta: Indian Publishing House, 1321 (B.S.), p. 168.
18. Mukhopadhaya, Prabhatkumar. *Gitabitān: kālānukramick suchi*. Calcutta: Tagore Research Institute, 1399 (B.S.), p. 26.
19. Tagore, Rabindranath. *Gitabitān. 3 Vols*. Calcutta: Visva-Bharati Granthan Vibhaga, 1338 (B.S.), p. 864.
20. Tagore. Rabindranath. *Valmiki Pratibha*. Calcutta: Adi Brahma Samaj, 1886. Contains: 25 songs of first edition, 7 songs of *Kalmrigya* and 21 new songs.
21. Tagore, Rabindranath. *Ganer Bahi O Valmiki Pratibha*. Calcutta: Adi Brahma Samaj, 1893. Contains: 218 songs of *Ganer Bahi*, 55 songs of *Valmiki Pratibha* and 150 songs of *Brahmasangit*.
22. Tagore, Rabindranath. *Karyagranthavali*. Calcutta: Santyendranath Gangyopadhaya, 1896. Contains: 16 songs of *Kaishorak*, 20 *Bhanusimghar Padavali*,2 *Chhabi O Gan*, 9 *Prakriter Pratisod*,10 *Kadi O Kamal*, 1 *Manasi*, 8 *Raja O Rani*, 1 *Chaitali*, 5 *Visarjan*, 3 *Sonar Tari*, 9 *Chitra*, 54 *Valmiki Pratibha*, 61 *Mayar Khela*, 119 *Gan*,162 *Brahmasangit*.
23. Tagore, Rabindranath. *Kabyagrantha*. Calcutta: Majumder Library, 1903. Total 442 songs, but 14 songs printed twice.
24. Tagore, Rabindranath. *Rabindragranthavali*. Calcutta: Hitabadi Library, 1904. Contains: 218 *Gaaner Bahi*, 54 *Valmiki Pratibha,149 Brahmasangit*.
25. Tagore, Rabindranath. *Gan*. Allahabad: Indian Press, 1908. Contains: 132 Various songs, 63 *Mayar Khela*,52 *Valmiki Pratibha*, 13 *National songs*, 20 *Baul*, 248 *Brahmasangit*.
26. Tagore, Rabindranath. *Prayaschitta*. Calcutta: Hitabadi Library, 1909. Includes 5 songs from *Bau-Thakuranir Hat*.
27. Tagore, Rabindranath. *Gan*. Calcutta: Indian Publishing House, 1914. Contains: 52 songs of *Valmiki Pratibha*, 63, *Mayar Khela*, 246 *Gan and* 34 *National Songs*.
28. Tagore, Rabindranath. *Dharmasangit*. Allahabad: Indian Press, 1914. It is rename of the *Gan* which includes all the *Brahmasangit*.
29. Tagore, Rabindranath. *Kavyagrantha-Vol. 10*. Allahabad: Indian Press, 1916. Contains: 52 *Valmiki Pratibha*, 33 *Mayar Khela*,120 Various Sangit, 220 *Dharmasangit*, 30 *National Songs*, 7 *Marriage Songs*.
30. Tagore, Rabindranath. *Ritu-uttsav*. Calcutta: Visva-Bharati Granthan Vibhaga, 1926. Contains: 24 *Seshbarshan*, 10 *Saraduttsav*, 23 *Basanta*, 24 *Sundar*, 27 *Phalguni*.

31. Mukhopadhaya, Prabhatkumar. *Gitabitan: kalanukramick suchi*. Calcutta: Tagore Research Institute, 1399 (B.S.), p. 31.
32. Tagore, Rabindranath. *Sangitchinta*. Calcutta: Visva-Bharati Granthan Vibhaga, 1399 (B.S.), p. 336.
33. Rabindranath gave the interview on Indian Poetry to Marguerite Wilkinson in New York. Published in *The Touchstone*, 7 (5),(Feb 1921).
34. Tagore, Rabindranath. *Jivansmriti*. Salaidaha: Nagendranath Gangyopadhaya, 1319,195 p. First edition corrected by Rabindranath kept in Rabindra Bhavan.
35. Tagore, Rabindranath. *Chhelebela*. Calcutta: Visva-Bharati Granthalaya, 1347, p. 87.
36. Thompson, E. *Rabindranath Tagore: Poet and Dramatist*. Calcutta: Rddhi-India, 1979; p. 30.
37. Ghose, Sisirkumar. *Rabindranath Tagore*. New Delhi: Sahitya Akademi, 1998, p. 32.
38. Thompson, E. *Rabindranath Tagore: Poet and Dramatist*. Calcutta: Rddhi-India, 1926, p. 61.
39. Kundu, A.K. *Rabindra-dinopanji*. Calcutta: Banglabhasha Sahityo O Samskriti Gabashana Samsthan, 1986. p. 399.
40. Tagore, Rathindranath. Father as I know him. In *Rabindranath Tagore: A centenary volume 1861-1961*. New Delhi: Sahitya Akademi, 1986, pp. 48-58.
41. Tagore, Rathindranath. The place of music in Education and culture, *The Visva-Bharati Quarterly*, 13 (1-2),(1947) 45.

Six

Letters of Rabindranath Tagore: A Bibliometric Study

Introduction

Rabindranath Tagore is essentially known to the world as a poet. But he was a great short-story writer, dramatist and novelist, a powerful author of essays and lectures, philosopher, composer and singer, innovator in education and rural development, actor, director, painter, cultural ambassador. Rabindranath wrote as many as 4098[1] letters from October 1978 to July 1941 which forms a substantial part of Tagoreana (all the intellectual output of Rabindranath). Besides family members, estate workers and Santiniketan associates Rabindranath wrote to literary personalities, poets like W.B. Yeats, Ezra Pound, artists, editors, thinkers like Romain Rolland, Bertrand Russell, scientist, educationist, scholars of Indian religion and philosophy, religious leaders, agricultural economist (Leonard Elmhurst), politicians and statesman like Mahatma Gandhi, Jawaharlal Nehru and Subhash Chandra Bose.

Rabindranath wrote huge number of letters during his lifetime not only to communicate messages to persons for specific purpose but also to express his ideas on nationalism, civilization, nature, society, education, *Swadeshi* movement and so on. So, the letters of Rabindranath helps to understand Tagore as a family man and also as a universal man with his many faceted vision and activities.

Tagore's letters written to his niece Indira Devi Chaudhurani published in *Chhinapatravali*[2] written during 1885-1895 are not just letters but finer prose where from the true picture of poet Rabindranath as well as imaginative Rabindranath can be drawn. Rabindranath wrote to W.B. Yeats "...I feel sure these letters, when published, will present to you pictures and ideas concerning me and my surroundings more vividly and truly than anything I have yet written"[3]. Most of the letters were first published in different journals and were in the personal collection of different people to whom the poet wrote. Only after the establishment of Rabindra Bhavana, Visva-Bharati took initiatives to collect them and later on publish in the book entitled *Chithipatra*[4]. It is a rare example in Indian literature, particularly in Bengali literature where manuscript of such a good number of letters are preserved and published. Letters written to Mahatma Gandhi[5], letters of English poets to Rabindranath[6], selected letters of Rabindranath[7] etc. have been published separately.

Objective of the Study

- To study the growth pattern of Rabindra Patrabali;
- To find out the persons to whom Rabindranath had written letters;
- To identify major themes of the letters; and
- To find out whether Rabindranath's letters follow any bibliometric law (Bradford's law).

Methodology

Bibliometric techniques are used "to analyse quantitatively the properties and behaviour of recorded knowledge"[8]. In this study statistical bibliometric technique is followed as it helps to "... shed light on the process of written communication and of the nature and course of development of discipline by means of counting and analyzing the various facets of written communication"[9].

Chithipatra, the book containing of Rabindranath's 4098 letters of Rabindranath was consulted. Original letters whenever necessary were consulted from Tagorean research centre and Rabindra Bhavana[10] museum to record the name of addresses, date of writing etc. Besides, primary and secondary sources in the form of original works or first editions of Tagore's work kept in Rabindra Bhavana were consulted. A wide range of secondary sources in the form of books and articles both in Bengali and English were consulted to corroborate and critically evaluate for the purpose of interpretation.

Analysis

Growth of Letters

Rabindranath composed his first poem at the age of eight and by the end of his life, he has written twenty-five volumes of poetry, fifteen plays, ninety-five short stories, eleven novels, thirteen volumes of essays; initiated and edited various journals; prepared Bengali textbooks, penned thousands of letters; and by the age of seventy created more than two thousand paintings. All these writings and paintings come under preview of Tagoreana.

Record of growth pattern of letters of Rabindranath may help to identify place of letters in Tagoreana. It may also help to know Tagore's imaginative thinking to construct his biography, to establish his relationship with different people, period of letter correspondence, mode of relationship, etc. Many letters may still be in the custody of individual correspondents. There are 4098 Rabindra Patrabali (letters) published in *Chithipatra.* The growth pattern of letters being substantial part of Tagoreana can be found from the following Table 6.1.

Rabindranath wrote all the first five letters in October 1878 to Kadambari Devi (wife of elder brother Jyotirindranath Tagore) from United Kingdom and the last letter to Pratima Devi (wife of poet's son Rathindranath Tagore) on 30th July, 1941 from Calcutta. The first verse narrative *Kavi-Kahini* published in 1878 and the final year (1941) of poet's departure from this 'earthly heaven' is marked with five publications, namely: *Arogya* (verse), *Janmadine* (verse), *Galpasalpa* (Stories and poems), *Sabhyatar Samkat* (address) and *Asramer Rup o Vikas* (essays). Rabindranath wrote highest number

Table 6.1: Growth of Rabindra Letters

Year	Jan.	Feb.	March	April	May	June	July	Aug.	Sept.	Oct.	Nov.	Dec.	Total
1878										5			5
1879													7(7)
1880	1												1
1881													1(1)
1882							1						1
1883	3		6									3	12
1884	1	1											12(10)
1885							1		1	3		2	11(4)
1886	2			1	2		2						35(28)
1887		1		1			1		2	2			7
1888				2		1							4(1)
1889				1		1						1	4(1)
1890	3				2	2		1	2	2		1	13
1891	9	8	1			10	2	4	3	5	1	1	45(1)
1892	3	1	1	2	11	12	7	2	1		1	10	55(4)
1893		9	5	4	6	3	9	4	2	1			43
1894		2	6	1		6	10	16	11	16	5	5	78
1895	1	9	11	7	1	5	6	6	5	8	5	9	73
1896			1							1			2
1897								1					2(1)
1898						2	2				1		4
1899				1	1	6	5	5	7	2	3	3	36(3)
1900		1	1	1	2	4	8	16	7	4	3	9	56
1901	4	3	17	10	10	6	7	7	4	2	3		74(1)
1902	1	6	2	14	8	1	3	2	2	3	4	4	50
1903	6	4	11	6	7	5	6	15	1	10	3	5	84(5)
1904	3	2	5	5	7	6	5	7	4	6	7		58(1)
1905			2	3	4	2	4	3		4	1	2	26(1)
1906	1	2	3	5	4	6	3			6	3	1	34
1907		1	1	5	8	2	4	4	6	10	5	15	63(2)
1908	14	17	10	8	6	3	9	3	6	3	7	4	90
1909	2		4	10	3		6	2	4	8	5	6	52(2)
1910	3	2	2	10	8	3	10	6	10	9	7	4	77(3)
1911	7	3	4	10	17	13	6	7	12	17	23	3	125(3)
1912	8	12	18	7	11	11	1	9	11	14	13	15	130
1913	21	16	10	11	20	5	4	2	2	5	12	5	115(2)
1914	4	6	9	9	7	5	8	2	5	4	1	4	70(6)
1915	4	10	10	4		4	6	5	4	4	5	5	66(5)
1916	9	13	4	13	8	3	4	6	7	7			74
1917			4	10	5	6	2	9	5	11	13	2	70(3)
1918	5	11	3	8	7	1	9	7	9	10	8	11	89
1919	3	3	2	12	12	4	6	5	2	8	10	5	74(2)
1920	6	5	2	1	2	2	3	7	4	2	2	4	40
1921	1	1	4	4	6	1	2	2	13	7	6	3	54(4)
1922	5	5	11	7	10	5	3	2	7	3	4		64(2)
1923	1	2	5	3	2	2	2	2	8	6	5	2	41(1)

(Contd.)

Table 6.1 (*Contd.*)

Year	*Jan*	*Feb.*	*March*	*April*	*May*	*June*	*July*	*Aug.*	*Sept.*	*Oct.*	*Nov.*	*Dec.*	*Total*
1924	2	3	3	4	2			2	7	2	1	7	34(1)
1925	2		3	9	8	4	3	1	5	9	4	8	57(1)
1926	5		1	7	8	3	4		1	5	1	14	52(3)
1927	16	5	14	9	10	6	14	14	13	9	19	12	144(3)
1928	7	18	4	6	8	5	13	17	20	23	12	5	138
1929	5	4	14	1		1	15	12	15	15	19	8	109
1930	7	13	2	5	9	5	7	7	7	20	5	1	88
1931	1	8	10	21	25	26	22	19	14	23	12	14	197(2)
1932	13	10	8	2		12	9	11	7	19	14	8	114(1)
1933	3	3	4	8	5	10	11	7	10	11	13	2	87
1934	10	1	11	22	7	5	12	15	6	18	6	6	119
1935	19	2	18	16	17	21	11	12	14	23	8	7	168
1936	10	6	4	14	5	9	12	6	15	28	5	9	123
1937	9	4	13	9	17	5	12	12	4	20	12	5	124(2)
1938	13	12	12	11	33	14	10	12	19	21	12	11	180
1939	9	8	14	9	11	9	9	5	12	19	7	3	117(2)
1940	11	8	9	7	16	7	6	6	5	3	2	4	84
1941	3	2	3	8	10	9	1						36

* Number within bracket in the total column indicates letter written in the corresponding year without any reference to the month or date.

of letters (N=197) in the year 1932 along with four Bengali books entitled *Parisesh* (verse), *Kaler Yatra* (drama), *Punascha* (prose-poem) and *Visvavidyalayer Rup* (essays) and two English titles *The Golden Boat* (poems) and *Mahatmaji and the Depressed Humanity* (address).

A listing of top recipients of the letters of Rabindranath with the dates of the first and the last letter might be of help for further study in this respect (*see* Table 6.2).

An in-depth study of all the letters written to top recipients may cast new lights in respect of Tagore's personal relationship with them, many facets of communicating and/or exchanging ideas etc. A listing of top themes on which Tagore corresponded is relevant in this respect.

It may be concluded from Table 6.3 that Tagore's concern about Santiniketan Ashram got top priority in his letters. Tagore's religious thinking and idea about the supreme can also be traced out from his letters.

Table 6.2: Top Ten Recipients

Sl. No.	*Name*	*Relationship with Rabindranath Tagore and/or his associates.*	*Date of Writing First-Last letter*	*No. of letters*
1.	Nirmal Kumari Mahalanobis[11]	Wife of Rabindra-associate Prasanta Chandra Mahalanobis.	22.4.1925—8.6.1941	506
2.	Indira Devi Chaudhurani[12]	Musician, translator and close companion of Rabindranath.	16.9.1887—13.5.1941	339
3.	Hemantabala Devi[13]	A great admirer of Rabindranat.	8.2.1931—10.5.1940	265
4.	Priyanath Sen[14]	Close friend of Rabindranat.	1881—1915	199
5.	Pramathanath Choudhuri[15]	Friend and admirer of Rabindranath.	21.5.1890—22.7.1940	137
6.	Ramananda Chattopadhyay[16]	Editor.	25.6.1910—14.6.1941	120
7.	Rathindranath Tagore[17]	Son.	14.5.1903—24.4.1940	111
8.	Manoranjan Bandyopadhyay[18]	Teacher of Santiniketan.	25.5.1902—14.6.1940	103
9.	Kadambini Devi[19]	Wife of Prangopal Dutta.	1.10.1903—10.5.1931	95
10.	Mira Devi[20]	Third daughter of Rabindranath.	5.2.1907—14.4.1938	83

Table 6.3: Top Ten Themes

S. No.	*Theme*	*Date of Writing of First-Last letter on the Theme*	*No. of Letters*
1.	Santiniketan Ashram	21.5.1890—11.6.1940	792
2.	Personal and family affairs	Jan 1883—30.7.1941	784
3.	God and religion	July 1886—18.12.1940	296
4.	Rathindranath (Son)	12.6.1889—Aug 1940	234
5.	Silaidaha (family estate)	1886—7.6.1939	160
6.	England (Travel)	Octo. 1878—6.51941	122
7.	Pratima Devi (Daughter-in-law)	27.1.1910—20.9.1940	112
8.	Reunite (Political issues)	Oct. 1878—16.5.1940	111
9.	Sangit (Music)	18.1.1891—21.3.1941	100
10.	Meera Devi (Daughter)	27.6.1898—26.7.1935	87

Bradford's Law

"Bradford's law of scattering"[21] states that journals in a single field can be divided into three categories, each containing same number of articles: (1) a core journals on the subject few in number, produces approximately one-third of the articles, (2) in second zone, containing the same number of articles as the first, but a greater number of journals, and (3) third zone, containing the same number of articles as the second, but still greater number of journals. This mathematical relationship of the number of journals in the core to the first zone is a constant n and in the second zone the relationship is n^2. Bradford expressed this relationship as $1:n:n^2$ (*see* Table 6.4).

This law can be applied in case of Tagore's letter to identify core persons with whom Tagore had more correspondence. Tagore wrote 4098 letters to 315 persons. His letters can be divided into the following three zones, each zone comprising more or less equal number of letters, i.e. one-third of the total number of letters (*see* Table 6.5).

Tagore wrote 1309 letters (1/3 of 4098 letters = 1366 letters) to 4 persons namely: Nirmal Kumari Mahalanobis, Indira Devi Chaudhurani, Hemantabala Devi and Priyanath Sen forming the first zone. In the second zone Tagore made his correspondence (N= 1377) to nineteen persons[22] and the remaining 1412 letters to 292 persons. According to the law the number of recipients in the third zone should have been 64 (4:16:64), Here, it is 292. Hence,

Table 6.4: Cumulative Total of the Letters

Recipients according to rank	*No. of letters*	*Cumulative total*
1	506	506
2	339	845
3	265	1110
4	199	1309
5	137	1446
6	120	1566
7	111	1677
8	103	1780
9	95	1875
10	83	1958
11-12	81 (written to 2 persons)	2120
13	73	2193
14	64	2257
15	63	2320
16	53	2373
17-18	50 (written to 2 persons)	2473
19	46	2519
20	44	2563
21	43	2606
22-23	40 (written to 2 persons)	2686
24	38	2724
25	37	2761
26	36	2797
27	35	2832
28	32	2864
29-31	30 (written to 3 persons)	2954
32	29	2983
33	27	3010
34	26	3036
35-36	25 (written to 2 persons)	3086
37	24	3110
38	21	3131
39-41	20 (written to 3 persons)	3191
42-43	18 (written to 2 persons)	3227
44-46	17 (written to 3 persons)	3278
47-48	16 (written to 2 persons)	3310
49	15	3325
50-53	14 (written to 4 persons)	3389
54-55	13 (written to 2 persons)	3415
56-57	12 (written to 2 persons)	3439
58-62	11 (written to 5 persons)	3494

(*Contd.*)

Table 6.4 *(Contd.)*

Recipients according to rank	*No. of letters*	*Cumulative total*
63-66	10 (written to 4 persons)	3534
67-70	9 (written to 5 persons)	3570
71-73	8 (written to 3 persons)	3594
74-85	7 (written to 12 persons)	3678
86-92	6 (written to 7 persons)	3720
93-98	5 (written to 6 persons)	3750
99-109	4 (written to 11 persons)	3875
110-136	3 (written to 27 persons)	3963
137-180	2 (written to 44 persons)	3972
181-315	1 (written to 137 persons)	4098

Table 6.5: Distribution of Letters According to the Zones

Zone	*No. of letters*	*Recipients*
First	1309	4
Second	1377	19
Third	1412	292

it cannot be said the number of letters strictly follow Bradford's law.

Discussion

Tagore's long literary career has been classified by different scholars from different viewpoint of literary development. Chunkapura classified it as youth and early adulthood writings (1878-1900), *Gitanjali* period (1900-1912), the years of matured reflections (1912-1927) and the final years (1927-1941)[23]. Thompson classified development of Tagoreana as early life and poetry (1861-1886), The *Shileida* and *Sadhana* period (1887-1897), unrest and change (1898-1905), *Gitanjali* period (1905-1919) and finally internationalism (1919-1941)[24]. Majumdar leaving aside the period of radiant dawn 1875-1880, before the rise of the effulgent sun, divided the literary life of the poet into four epochs. The first period covers seventeen years from 1881-1897, from the date of writing of *Bau Thakuranir Hat* to that of composing the *Lakshmir Pariksha*. The second period is that of full maturity extending from 1898 to

1913. The next thirteen years or third period from 1914 to 1926 may be called the age of rejuvenation of the poet and his revolt against the conventional society. The last period covering fifteen years, 1927 to 1941 is the age of glorious and picturesque sunset[25]. Tagore's biographer Prabhat Kumar Mukhopadhyaya though not categorically distinguished writings of Tagore like others but pointed out different phases of life such as 'littérateur in the making', 'the flower blossoms', 'the humanitarian takes his stand'; 'the nationalist takes shape', 'the brotherhood of man', 'the diffusion of culture'[26]. Kripalani pointed out different phases as adolescence, youth, maturity, a man among men, a world citizen, world in one nest, old world and new, between two worlds[27]. It is evident from the growth of letters that Tagore wrote letters throughout his literary career. Highest productivity (N=1818) can be observed in the final or glorious and picturesque sunset years (1927-1941). It is obvious that the growth of Tagoreana with the passage of time reflected faithfully the diverse tendencies of his age. But at the same time these help to usher in a new epoch in Indian history.

Conclusion

It is clear from the study that *Rabindra Patrabali* as a literary form/forms a substantial part of Tagoreana. Tagore used his mighty pen to write huge number of letters not only as a medium of personal communication but to express his ideas on different aspects of life/society or even travel account. His concerns about Santiniketan ('abode of peace') amply are reflected in his letters. An in-depth study of letters reveals that many times tagore used letters to draft his ideas of short stories or even poems. For example, characters of his short stories like '*Giribala of 'Megh o Raudra*', '*Postmaster*', *Mrinmayi of 'Samapti'* or *Phatik of 'Chhuti'* make their first appearance in letters[28].

Rabindra Patrabali does not strictly follow Bradford's law. But it helps to identify core personalities to whom Rabindranath made maximum letters correspondence, particularly in respect of first and second zone. Content analysis of these letters may open new vistas of Tagorean research.

Notes and References

1. Number of published letters. There may be unpublished letters in the personal custody, scattered all over the world. Majority of the published letters are kept at Tagore's Museum Rabindra Bhavana.
2. Tagore, Rabindranath. *Chhinapatravali*. Calcutta: Visva-Bharati Granthan Vibhaga, 1961, p. 242.
3. Dutta, Krishna and Robinson, Andrew. *Selected letters of Rabindranath Tagore*. Cambridge: Cambridge University Press, 1997, p. 209. Rabindranath Tagore's letter to W.B. Yeats dated 17th June 1918.
4. Tagore, Rabindranath. *Chithipatra*-19 Vols. Calcutta: Visva-Bharati Granthan Vibhaga, 1976.
5. Bhattacharya, Sabyasachi. *Mahatma and the Poet: Letters and debates between Gandhi and Tagore1915-1941*. New Delhi: National Book Trust, 1997, p. 216.
6. Chakravarty, Bikash. *Poets to poets 1912-1940: Letters from Bridges, Rhys, Yeats, Sturge Moore, Trevelyan and Pound*. Calcutta: Visva-Bharati, 1998, p. 286.
7. Dutta, Krishna and Robinson, Andrew. *Selected letters of Rabindranath Tagore*. Cambridge: Cambridge University Press, 1997, p. 561.
8. Pritchard, A., Statistical bibliography or bibliometrics, *Journal of Documentation*. 24(4) (1969) 348.
9. Hulme, E.W. *Statistical bibliography in relation to the growth of modern civilization*. London: Grafton, London, 1923, p. 44.
10. Rabindranath entered in the first house in present Uttarayan complex on 14/15 Dec,1919, made of mad, covered with hatched and named it Uttarayan. The present changed structured of that house is Konark. At present the entire complex has five houses (Udayan, Konark, Shyamali, Punascha and Udichi) made during Rabindranath's life time, and Vichitra constructed in the centenary year (1961) of Rabindranath as Tagore Research Centre (Rabindra Bhavana) is known as Uttarayan Complex.
11. Nirmal Kumari ('Rani') Mahalanobis (Maitra) (1900-1981): wife of Prasanta Chandra Mahalanobis and daughter of Heramba Chandra Maitra.
12. Indira Devi Chaudhurani (1373-1960): Musician, translator and close companion of Rabindranath from 1878; daughter of Satyendranath Tagore, husband of Pramatha Chaudhuri. She gave many notations of Rabindranath's songs.

13. Hemantabala Devi (Ray) (1894-1975): Having admired a Tagore novel, *Yogayog*, she began corresponding with Rabindranath under various pseudonyms. Inspired by Tagore she became a writer.
14. Priyanath Sen (1854-1916): Close friend and literary companion of Rabindranath.
15. Pramathanath Choudhuri (1868-1946): Editor of *Shabuj Patra*, essayist, short-story writer; he married Indira Devi Chaudhurani. He was a friend, an admirer but not a discipline of Rabindranath.
16. Ramananda Chattopadhyay (1865-1943): Journal editor; founded *Prabashi* (1901) and *Modern Review* (1907).
17. Rathindranath Tagore (1888-1961): Son of Rabindranath Tagore; trained in agriculture science in USA, he helped Tagore to manage his states and became Visva-Bharati's administrator.
18. Manoranjan Bandyopadhyay (1871-1950): Joined as teacher of Santiniketan Ashram in 1309 Asad (B.S) (1902-03). He was given special responsibility to prepare "Rathi" (Rathindranath Tagore) for Entrance examination.
19. Kadambini Devi: Daughter of Mohim Chandra Sankar; Wife of Prangopal Dutta.
20. Mira Devi (Gangulee) (1894-1969): Third daughter of Rabindranath; married Nagendranath Gangulee.
21. Bradford, S.C. Sources of Information on specific subjects, *Engineering*, 26 (1934) 85-86.
22. Besides the six names mentioned in Table 6.2 (Sl. No. 5-10) remaining nine correspondents in second zone are: Amiya Chakravarty (81), Bhupendranath Sanyal (81), Pratima Devi (73), Dilipkumar Ray (64), Ranu Mookerjii (63), Mohitchandra Sen (53), Ajit Kumar Chakraborty (50), Amal Home (50), Dineshchandra Sen (46), Srischandra Mazumder (44), Jagadananda Roy(43), Monilal Gangyopadhyaya(40), Nagendranath Gangulee(40). [Number within bracket indicates letter number].
23. Chunkapura, Jose. *The God of Rabindranath Tagore: A study of the evolution of his understanding of God.* Calcutta: Visva-Bharati Granthan Vibhaga, 2002, p. 351.
24. Thompson, Edward. *Rabindranath Tagore: Poet and dramatis.* Calcutta: Rddhi-India, 1979, p. 335.
25. Majumdar, Bimanbehari. *Heroines of Tagore: A study in the transformation of Indian society 1875-1941.* Calcutta: Firma K.L. Mukhopadhyay, 1968, p. 15.

26. Mukhopadhyaya, Prabhat Kumar. *Life of Tagore*. New Delhi: Indian Book Company, 1975, p. 208. Tr. from Bengali by Sisirkumar Ghosh.
27. Kripalani, Krishna. *Rabindranath Tagore: A biography*. Calcutta: Visva-Bharati Granthan Vibhaga, 1980, p. 491.
28. Mitra, Somnath. *The letters of Rabindranath Tagore*; in *Rabindranath Tagore: A centenary volume 1861-1961*, New Delhi: Sahitya Akademi, 1986, pp. 163-171.

Seven
Gitanjali: A Bibliometric Study

Introduction

Gitanjali in Bengali was published in September 1910 with 157 songs and poems. Out of these songs 20 were previously published in *Shārodutsav*[1] in 1908 and *Gān*[2] in 1909. The remaining 137 poems and songs were written in 90 days in between August 1909 to August 1910 (10th Bhadra 1316 to 29th Shravan 1317 (B.S.)[3]. Rabindranath Tagore himself took the task of the translation of *Gitanjali* (Song Offerings) when he sailed for England on 27th May 1912. There he handed over the poems to William Rothenstein whom he met earlier in Calcutta in the year 1911. Moved by the poems Rothenstein in turn gave the poems to W.B. Yeats to read. The literary and artistic circle of Yeats decided to publish the poems after Yeats made a selection of them and wished to write an introduction to it. That is how *Gitanjali* was first published by India Society of London on 1st November 1912. It was written in the half title page of the publication that "seven hundred and fifty copies of this edition have been printed for the India Society of which two hundred and fifty copies only are for sale"[4]. Regarding this Rabindranath wrote to Kshitimohan Sen "… I feel he must be happy with my writing and wants others to share that happiness. It is something like our taking delight in the lotus we offer him because he delights in it. I feel he has brought me from East to West…"[5]. Rabindranath got the Nobel Prize for literature on 13th November

1913 for *Gitanjali.* The recommendation within Swedish Academy came from another winner of the Nobel Prize-Werner von Heidenstam. He wrote that he had read no lyric writing to equal Tagore's in the previous twenty years or more. "They gave me hours of intense enjoyment; it was like drinking the water of a fresh, clear spring... There is nothing in his work that is controversial and offensive, nothing vain, worldly and petty, and if ever a poet may be said to possess the qualities that make him entitled to the Nobel Prize, it is he"[6]. *The Daily Mail* (Nov. 14, 1913; p. 7, Col 13) under the heading Nobel Prize for an Indian Poet quotes W.B. Yeats "I know of no man in my life time who has done anything in the English language equal to Mr. Tagore's lyrics"[7].

The next edition of *Gitanjali* was published in the next year (March 1913) by Macmillan and Company, London. The number of poems in Bengali and English *Gitanjali* are not the same. In Bengali there were 157 poems, but in English it was 103. The poems were first published in different *Kavyagrantha* (collection of poems). At the end of the Indian edition of India Society or Macmillan there was a statement: "These translations are of poems contained in three books—*Naivedya, Kheya* and *Gitanjali*—to be had at the Indian Publishing House, 22 Cornwallis Street, Calcutta; and of a few poems which have appeared in periodicals"[8]. But this information is not complete as the poems were collected from ten books (Table 7.1).

Even a comparative study of *Gitanjali* published by India Society, London and Macmillan edition besides punctuations, change can be noticed such as in poem number 52 one can observe in Indian Society edition

> *....no more coyness and sweetness of demeanor. (Page 47)*

But the same line in Macmillan edition has changed as:

> ...no more shy and soft demeanour.

These changes have been made comparing them with the manuscript and according to Yeats' suggestions. Even there were some mistakes in the first line of the content of India Society publication (the poem number and correct line is given in the bracket) such:

Prisoner, tell me, who it was (31);
(*Prisoner, tell me, who was it*);
Let only that little remain of me (34);
(*Let only that little be left of me*);
Hast thou not heard his silent steps? (45);
(*Have you not heard his silent steps?*);
When first they came out, the warriors (85);
(*When the warriors came out first*);
When I give up the helm, then the time has come (99);
(*When I give up the helm, I know that the time has come*).

Even by scientific comparison of original Bengali poems and English translation one can find,

(i) In the English translation number 61 of *Khoka* from *Shishu* the last two stanzas were deleted.
(ii) In the second line of translation number 71 "amar" has been translated as "thy" but actually it is "tomar".
(iii) The translated poem number 95 comprises two poems; complete poem number 89 of *Naivedya* and last stanza of 90th poem in Bengali,
(iv) Only the first part of the poem "*Utsarga*" has been translated in the English translation number 102.

Objectives

The study has the following major objectives:

- To trace the origin and growth pattern of the poems of *Gitanjali* in different *Kavyagrantha* (books of poems)
- To find out the use of words (homonyms, synonyms, etc.) and its repetition, and to know different literary connotations in the poems of *Gitanjali*.

- To find out the number of poems used as songs and their availability in *Swarabitan* (book of notation).
- To find out whether Gitanjali follows bibliometric laws (Zipf's law), and finally
- To justify poetic justice of the title '*Gitanjali*' with rank frequency distribution of words.

Methodology and Source

For bibliometric study of *Gitanjali* every poem of the source document in respect of its length, place and date of writings has been considered. Every word of the poems was also minutely studied and recorded to know the use of words, its repetition and also rank-frequency of every word calculated for verification of the bibliometric law (Zips law). For bibliometric study of *Gitanjali*, its bilingual edition published by Rabindra-Bhavan was consulted as the source document as Bengali poems of this edition has been taken from the last publication (1349 B.S.) of *Gitanjali* published during Tagore's life time and, as it is bilingual, so a comparative study is possible[9]. The editions of India Society and Macmillan were also consulted. *Gitabitan*[10] and all the volumes of *Swarabitan*[11] were also consulted to find out how many poems of *Gitanjali* are songs and are available in which volume of *Swarabitan* (Book of notations).

Gitanjali: A Bibliometric Studv

In fact, *Gitanjali* submitted for the Nobel Prize is a collection of 103 poems from ten other 'books of poems' published earlier. Table 7.1 indicates the poems taken from different 'books of poems' and their years of publication.

Poems of *Gitanjali* were written at different places even on the train, though majority of the poems were written at Bolpur-Santinketan (18 poems out of 52) where place of writing is mentioned.

Table 7.1: Poems of Gitanjali from Different Kavyagrantha

Sl. No.	*Book*	*Year of Publication*	*No of poems*
1.	*Chaitali*	1912	1
2.	*Kalpana*	1900	1
3.	*Naivedya*	1901	15
4.	*Smaran*	1903	1
5.	*Shishu*	1903	3
6.	*Utsarga*	1903	1
7.	*Kheya*	1906	11
8.	*Gitanjali*	1910	53
9.	*Achalayatan*	1912	1
10.	*Giti-malya*[12] *(collected from the manuscript for Gitanjali, before publication as book in 1914)*	1914	16
	Total		**103**

Table 7.2: Places of Writing of Poems of Gitanjali

Sl. No.	*Place*	*No. of Poems*	*%*
1.	Bolpur	11	10.680
2.	Santiniketan	7	6.796
3.	Silaidaha	13	12.621
4.	Calcutta	11	10.680
5.	Almorah	2	1.942
6.	Hampstead	2	1.942
7.	Kaya/Korai	1	0.970
8.	Tindhariya	1	0.970
9.	"Padma" on Boat	1	0.970
10.	Railway/E.I.R	1	0.970
11.	Giridi	1	0.970
12.	Jainpur/Gorai	1	0.970
13.	Not Mentioned	51	49.515
	Total	**103**	**100.00**

Rabindranath did not mention the places of writing in 51 poems of *Gitanjali*. Table 7.3 indicates the name and number of poems of the original *Kavyagrantha*.

From Table 7.3 it is clear that most of the poems where the place of writing is not mentioned are from original Bengali version of *Gitanjali* which contained 157 poems, out of which 53 poems were selected for English version of *Gitanjali* submitted for the Nobel Prize. In case of poem number 95 of *Gitanjali* (English version) two

Table 7.3: Poems where Place of Writing not Mentioned

Sl. No.	Kavyagrantha	No. of Poems	Serial No. of Poems in Gitanjali	%
1.	*Gitanjali*	29	2 (78), 3 (22), 6 (87), 9 (105), 10 (107), 15 (31), 17 (150), 28 (144), 29 (142), 30(103), 34 (138), 38 (88), 39 (58), 46 (34), 49 (56), 58 (134), 30 (59), 63 (3), 65 (101), 66(148), 74 (26), 77 (92), 79 (28), 83 (10), 84 (25), 96 (157), 97 (68), 132 (101), 103 (147)	56.863
2	*Naivedya*	15	4 (75), 25 (98), 35 (72), 36 (99), 40 (86), 43 (33), 67 (81), 69 (26), 73 (30), 75 (44), 76 (1), 79 (28), 82 (39), 86 (18), 95 (89&90)	29.411
3	*Kheya*	1	54	1.961
4	*Achalayatan*	1	57	1.961
5	*Shishu*	1	62	1.961
6	*Swaran*	1	87	1.961
7	*Kalpana*	1	88	1.961
8	*Chaitali*	1	92 (6)	1.961
9	*Utsarga*	1	102 (6)	1.961
	Total	**51**		**100.00**

* In the column of serial number of poems there are two numbers: first one indicates the number *Gitanjali* and the second one within first brackets indicates the poem number in original *Kavyagrantha* ('book of poems').

poems of *Naivedya* (number 89 and 90) were combined together. But in all the poems of *Gitanjali* dates of 103 poems are available as indicated in Table 7.4.

From Table 7.4 it is clear that most of the poems (69 out of 103) were written in the years 1910-13 just before the submission of *Gitanjali* to the Nobel Committee, on the other hand some poems were written long before even in the year of 1895. The length of the poems of *Gitanjali* would help to have an idea about the total number of lines and its percentage thereof.

From Table 7.5 it is clear that 30 poems (21.798%) are of 16 lines and 17 poems (10.808%) are of 15 lines.

Use of double or triple words in sentences as well as repetition of single word in lines indicates the literary stress on that word that is indicated in Tables 7.6 and 7.7 respectively. For example it can be observed from Table 7.6 that in poem number 10 of *Gitanjali* the word *Sabar* (for all) has been used four times to indicate 'the

Table 7.4: Dates of Writing of Poems of Gitanjali

Sl. No.	*Year*	*Year, Date*	*No. of Poems*
1.	1895	2nd April	1
2.	1901	1901 (1)	1
3.	1902	1902 (15)	15
4.	1903	1903 (1)	1
5.	1904	1904 (3), July/Aug, 23rd Aug	5
6.	1906-7	11th Aug, 14th Aug, 13th Sept, 15th Jan, 21st March, 24th March, 25th March.	7
7.	1907	17th June, 25th June	2
8.	1908	28th June	1
9.	1909	1909 (1)	1
10.	1910-11	7th April, June/July(3), July/Aug, 28th Aug, 30th Aug.(2), 31st Aug, 3rd Sept.(3), 5th Sept, 14th Sept, 18th Oct, 28th Dec. 10th April, 11th April	18
11.	1911	26th April,18th May, 1st June, 2nd June, 11th June, 13th June, 14th June, 18th June(2), 20th June, 28th June(2), 30th June, 4th July, 10th July, 11th July, 12th July, 13th July, 16th July(2), 18th July, 19th July, 26th July, 28th July, 1st Aug, 7th Aug,8th Aug(2), 9th Aug, 10th Aug,11th Aug(2), 15th Aug.	33
12.	1912	Aug/Sept, 23rd March, 1st April(2), 2nd April, 8th April, 9th April, 10th April(2), 11th April, 13th April, 14th April	12
13.	1913	20th April, 21st April(2), 23rd April, 24th June, 26th June	6
	Total		**103**

* The number within brackets indicates the number of poem written in that particular year, month.

Table 7.5: Length of Poems of Gitanjali

Sl. No.	*No. cf lines*	*Poem nos. in Gitanjali*	*No. of poems*	*Total lines*	*%*
1.	72	48	1	72	3.270
2.	60	51,52	2	120	5.450
3.	50	50,61	2	100	4.541
4.	48	41	1	48	2.180
5.	46	102	1	46	2.089
6.	40	47,60,66	3	120	5.450
7.	36	54,64,78	3	108	4.905
8.	33	80	1	33	1.499

(Contd.)

Sl. No.	No. of lines	Poem nos. in Gitanjali	No. of poems	Total lines	%
9.	32	71	1	32	1.453
10.	30	27	1	30	1.362
11.	28	31,88,91	3	84	3.815
12.	27	79	1	27	1.226
13.	25	55	1	25	1.135
14.	24	11,12	2	48	2.180
15.	22	13,103	2	44	1.998
16.	21	44,70	2	42	1.907
17.	20	6,8,9,14,17,18,47,49,62,62,74,85,86,89,96	15	300	13.624
18.	19	95	1	19	0.863
19.	18	10,56,59	3	54	2.452
20.	16	1,2,5,7,15,19,20,21,22,24,26,28,30,32,33,38 39,42,46,53,65,76,77,83,84,90,94,97,99,100	30	480	21.798
21.	15	25,72,73,101	4	60	2.725
22.	14	4,16,23,34,35,36,40,43,58,67,68,69,75,81, 82,87,92	17	238	10.808
23	12	3,29,37,57,93,98	6	72	3.270
	Total		**103**	**2202**	**100.00**

Table 7.6: Double/Triple Words Used in a Sentence or Part of a Sentence in Gitanjali

Sl. No.	Poem No.	Sentences	Poem lines	Double/Triple words	Frequency
1.	2	3	10	*Bhalo lage* (appears good to one)	1
2.	3	1, 4	2, 9	*Shuni* (listen), *Kaite* (to speak)	2
3.	6	4, 7	9, 19	*Chhinnakoro* (tear)	2
4.	10	1, 2, 3, 4	3, 9, 12, 17	*Sabar* (for all)	4
5.	11	6	17	*Mukti* (to be free from earthly bondage)	2
6.	16	2	2	*Dhanya holo* (became gratified)	1
7.	19	3	9	*Habe* (will be)	1
8.	27	1, 2, 12, 13	1, 2, 25, 26	*Alo Jwalo* (light up)	4
9.	38	1, 2	1, 7	*Chai* (desire)	2
10.	42	1	2, 4	*Bhese* (float), Kon deshe (in which country)	2
11.	45	1	1	*Ashe* (come)	1
12.	91	1, 3, 6, 9	2, 7,17, 27	*Maran* (death)	4
13.	103	1,2	1, 2, 7, 8, 13, 14, 19, 20	*Ekti namaskare* (in a single namaskar)	8

Table 7.7: Repetition of Single Word in a Sentence in Gitanjali

Sl. No.	*Poem no.*	*Line(s) in poems*	*Repeated word(s)*	*Fre-quency*
1.	2	3	*Chhalchhal* (tearfulness)	1
2.	13	13	*Kshane Kshane* (from moment to moment)	1
3.	14	7,15	*Dine Dine* (day by day), *Jani Jani* (know I know)	2
4.	16	9	*Gane Gane* (song to song)	1
5.	19	9	*Habe Habe* (will be, will be)	1
6.	23	6	*Bare Bar* (time and again)	1
7.	24	5	*Dhire Dhire* (slowly)	1
8.	27	14,17,18	*Jhari* (fall), *Mari* (die)	3
9.	28	10	*Rashi Rashi* (heaps of)	1
10.	30	3	*Sathe Sathe* (with)	1
11.	45	3	*Juge Juge* (era after era), *Pale Pale* (in moments)	2
12.	46	11,12	*Theke Theke* (at times), *Kenpe Kenpe* (treambling)	2
13.	66	15,22	*Chupe Chupe* (silently), *Deshe Deshe* (at home and abroad)	2
14.	70	5,8	*Dike Dike* (everywhere), *Dheye Dheye* (chasing and chasing)	2
15.	84	2,5,9	*Bhubane Bhubane* (at all places), *Taray Taray* (from star to star), *Ghare Ghare* (at every home)	3
16.	100	3	*Ghate Ghate* (from ghat to ghat)	1
17.	101	5	*Dware Dware* (from door to door)	2

Giti-Malya

1	1	4,7	*Naba Naba* (new and new), *Phire Phire* (again and again)	2
2	5	14	*Chokhe Chokhe* (constant watch)	1
3	12	5,22	*Benke Benke* (meandering), *Aachho Aachho* (definitely present)	2
4	20	5	*Majhe Majhe* (from time to time)	1
5	21	9	*Chalchaliye* (like the noise of running water)	1
6	44	15,16,17	*Kshane Kshane* (from moment to moment), *Mane Mane* (in mind), *Rahi Rahi* (at intervals)	3
7	53	2,4,14	*Taray Taray* (among the stars), *Barne Barne* (word by word)	3
8	55	21	*Paye Paye* (at every step)	1
9	68	9	*Naba Naba* (new and new), *Barane* (respectful reception)	2
10	72	13,15	Gopane Gopane (secretly), *Niti Niti* (always)	2
11	89	2,4	*Kshane Kshane* (from moment to moment), *Gane Gane* (in songs)	2
12	98	7	*Thare Thare* (in strata)	1

Naivedya

1	25	1,3	*Majhe Majhe (at intervals)*, *Til Til* (slowly)	2
2	35	7	*Deshe Deshe*, *Dishe Dishe* (everywhere)	2
3	40	8,10	*Pale Pale* (at every moment), *Sanghara Sanghara* (destroy, destroy)	2
4	43	12	*Theke Theke* (at intervals)	1
5	67	67	*Nai Nai* (non-existence)	1
6	69	1,5,6,7,11	*Shiray Shiray* (in veins), *Chupe Chupe* (secretly), *Laksha Laksha* (in laskhs), *Trine Trine* (in every grass), *Barashe Barashe* (year after year), *Ange Ange* (in limbs).	6
7	81	1,5	*Majhe Majhe* (at intervals), *Antare Antare* (in hearts)	2
8	82	11	*Dite Dite* (giving)	1

Kheya

1	41	25	*Cheye Cheye* (observing)	1
2	48	4,19	*Bhare Bhare* (large quantity), *Ghure Ghure* (continious traveling)	2
3	50	2,3,19,20	*Pathe Pathe* (on roads), *Dware Dware* (from door to door), *Mutha Mutha* (handful), *Bhare Bhare*.	4
4	51	15,25,28	*Ghare Ghare* (in homes), *Kshane Kshane*, *Jhanjhani* (noise of striking a thin metal)	3
5	78	8	*Dale Dale* (in flocks)	1
6	80	14,17	*Naba Naba*, *Barne Barne*	2

Shishu

1	61	32, 40	*Ghire Ghire* (surrounding)	2
2	62	8	*Patay Patay* (in leaves)	1

Achalayatan

1	57	9,10	*Majhe Majhe*, *Patay Patay*	2

Kalpana

1	88	2,4	*Theke Theke*, *Phire Phire*	2

Chaitali

1	92	6	*Ghare Ghare*	1

Utsarga

1	102	9, 25, 26, 35	*Ki Jani, Ki Jani* (not sure), *Kshane Kshane*	4

poorest, and lowliest, and lost' or in poem number 91 the word *Maran* (death) has been used four times as the poet prayed for the '*last fulfilment of life, Death, my death, come and whisper to me*'.[13].

Rabindranath many a time used polysemous words in a sentence with different literary connotations in his poems as indicated in Tables 7.8 and 7.9 respectively.

Table 7.8: Use of Pair of Contrasting Words in a Line

Gitanjali				
Sl. No.	*Poem No.*	*Line(s) in Poems*	*Contrasting pair of words*	*Frequency*
1	11	13	*Roudra Jale* (In sun and in shower)	1
2	13	16	*Aasa Jaoa* (come-and-go)	1
3	16	10	*Kanna Hasi* (tears and smiles)	1
4	17	16	*Becha Kena* (Buying and selling)	1
5	28	1	*Jaraya Chharaya* (In trammel and in break)	1
6	29	3	*Dibarati* (Day and night, All the times)	1
7	34	5	*Dibanishi* (Day and night, All the times)	1
8	38	6	*Dine Rate* (During day and night, All the times)	1
9	45	3	*Din-Rajani* (Day and night, All the times)	1
10	46	5	*Sakal-Sanjhe* (In morning and evening)	1
11	58	6	*Jiban-Maran* (Life and death)	1
12	63	3,11,7	*Dur Nikat* (Distant and near), *Nutan Puratan* (Old and new), *Jiban Maran* (Life and dealth)	5 (*Dur Nikat* used thrice)
13	66	23	*Bhanga Gara* (Destruction and creation)	1
14	74	12	*Aasa Jaoa* (coming and going)	1
15	77	12	*Sukhe Dukhe* (In pleasure and pain)	1
16	84	12	*Sukhe Dukhe*	1
17	90	8,12	*Sandhya Prabhat* (Evening and morning, All the times), *Duhkho Sukh* (Pain and pleasure)	2
18	91	6	*Duhkho Sukh*	1
19	101	12	*Duhkho Sukh*	1
20	103	18	*Dibasratri* (Day and night, All the time)	1

Table 7.8 (*Contd.*)

			Naivedya	
1	4	2	*Rajani Dibas* (Day and night, All the times)	1
2	25	14	*Ratri Dibas* (Day and night, All the times)	1
3	35	3	*Dibas Sharbari* (Day and night, All the times)	1
4	36	5	*Sukhe Dukhe*	1
5	43	9	*Sukh Duhkha*	1
6	69	2,9,10	*Ratri Din (Night and day), Janma-mrityu* (birth and death), *Joar-vanta* (in ebb and flow)	3
7	82	2	*Ratri Din*	1
8	95	9	*Sukhe Dukhe*	1
			Kheya	
1	31	21	*Rajani Din* (Night and day)	1
2	41	9,19	*Sakal-Sandhya* (Morning and evening)	2
3	48	11	*Dahin-banya* (Right-left)	1
4	78	27	*Dine Ratre* (In day and night)	1
			Giti-Malya	
1	44	3, 7	*Roudra Chhaya* (light and shadow), *Aase Jay* (Come and go)	2
2	71	11, 14, 19, 27, 31	*Kanna Hasi* (Tears and smiles), *Bhange Gare* (destroy and create), *Dibanishi* (Day and night), *Dure Kache* (Far and near), *Jaoa Aasa* (going and coming)	5
3	72	7	*Sukhe Dukhe*	1
4	89	6, 15	*Becha Kena (Selling and buying), Manda Bhalo* (Evil and good)	2
			Shishu	
1	61	4,10	*Jaoa Aasa* ((Hide and seek)	2
			Chaitali	
1	92	6	*Sukhe Dukhe*	1

Table 7.9: Use of Contrasting Pair of Words in a Sentence

Sl. No.	*Poem No.*	*Line(s) in Poems*	*Contrasting pair of word(s)*	*Frequency*
			Gitanjali	
1	37	4	*Puratan Nutan* (Old and new)	1
2	39	4	*Kripan Udar* (Miserly Noble)	1
3	45	6	*Dukhe Sukhe*	1
4	83	5	*Dite Nite* (to give or to take)	1

Table 7.9 (*Contd.*)

			Naivedya	
1	73	2	*Bandhan Mukti* (Bond and freedom)	1
2	95	1	*Jiban Mrityu* (Life and death)	1
			Kheya	
1	31	7	*Swadhin Das* (Free and bonded)	1

Actually many poems of Rabindranath are songs, and poems of *Gitanjali* are no exception. Table 7.10 justifies this statement as 42 out of 103 poems are songs of which notations are scattered in different volumes of *Swarabitan* (book of notations) published by Visva-Bharati.

Table 7.10: Poems of Gitanjali that are Songs

Sl. No.	*Poem No.*	*Notation first published by Visva-Bharati*	*Volume in Swarabitan*
1.	1	Gitalekha Vol. 1/1324-27 (B.S)	39
2.	3	Gitanjali/1927	38
3.	5	Gitalipi-vol. 6/1910-18	39
4.	10	Gitanjali/1927	38
5.	13	Gitalipi-vol. 2/1910-18	38
6.	14	Brahmasangit-vol. 5/1311-18 (B.S)	24
7.	15	Gitalipi-vol. 2/1910-18	38
8.	16	Gitalipi-vol. 5/1910-18	37
9.	18	Gitalipi-vol. 3/1910-18	37
10.	21	Gitalekha-vol. 1/1324-27 (B.S)	39
11.	22	Gitalipi-vol. 3/1910-18	11
12.	23	Gitalipi-vol. 3/1910-18	11
13.	26	Gitalipi-vol. 5/1910-18	38
14.	27	Gitalipi-vol. 6/1910-18	11
15.	28	Gitalipi-vol. 5/1910-18	37
16.	39	Gitalipi-vol. 5/1910-18	38
17.	44	Gitalekha-vol. 3/1324-27 (B.S)	41
18.	45	Gitalipi-vol. 3/1910-18	38
19.	46	Gitalipi-vol. 1/1910-18	37
20.	49	Gitalipi-vol. 5/1910-18	37
21.	53	Gitanjali/1927	42
22.	55	Gitalekha/1324-27 (B.S)	39
23.	56	Gitalipi-vol. 4/1910-18	37
24.	57	Gitanjali/1927	52
25.	59	Gitalipi-vol. 3/1910-18	38
26.	63	Brahmasangit-vol. 6/1311-18 (B.S)	26
27.	65	Gitalipi-vol. 4/1910-18	38
28.	70	Gitalipi-vol. 2/1910-18	38

(*Contd.*)

Table 7.10 *(Contd.)*

Sl. No.	*Poem No.*	*Notation first published by Visva-Bharati*	*Volume in Swarabitan*
29.	72	Gitalekha vol. 2/1324-27 (B.S)	40
30.	74	Gitalipi vol. 3/1910-18	38
31.	76	Brahmasangit vol. 4/1311-18 (B.S)	24
32.	77	Gitalipi vol. 5/1910-18	37
33.	79	Gitalipi vol. 1/1910-18	38
34.	83	Gitanjali/1917	50
35.	84	Gitalekha vol. 2/1324-27 (B.S)	37
36.	89	Gitalekha vol. 1/1324-27 (B.S)	39
37.	93	Gitalipi vol. 6/11910-18	40
38.	94	Gitanjali/1917	41
39.	97	Gitalipi vol. 3/1910-18	37
40.	98	Gitalekha vol. 1/1324-27 (B.S)	39
41.	100	Gitalipi vol. 1/1910-18	38
42.	103	Gitanjali/1917	38

According to Zipf's law, the conspicuousness [i.e. rank] or intensity of any element [i.e. word] of language is inversely proportional to its frequency. Using X for frequency and Y for rank, the law can be stated as $Y \alpha 1/X = > N$, where N is a constant. Frequency of words occurring in *Gitanjali* and their corresponding ranks are given in Table 7.11. For example, the word *amar* (*my*) has occurred 1740 times, *tomar* (your) 467 times, and so on.

Table 7.11: Rank-Frequency of Words Occurring in Gitanjali

Rank (Y)	*Frequency (X)*	*Constant (N)*
1	1740	1740
2	467	934
3	238	714
4	139	556
5	100	500
6	65	390
7	51	357

Conclusion

From the above analysis of *Gitanjali* it may be concluded that:

(i) The first poem of *Gitanjali* was written in 1895 and the last poem in 1913. The maximum number of poems (33) was written in 1911. Thus, it appears that Rabindranath never wrote the poems of *Gitanjali* consciously for Nobel Prize purpose.

(ii) From the available dates it is found that Rabindranath wrote 17.476 per cent poems at Bolpur-Santiniketan where Tagore established his experimental school.

(iii) Most of the poems (21.798%) are of 16 lines and 52.27 per cent poems are of 14 to 20 lines.

(iv) Rabindranath used double or triple words on 33 occasions, repetition of single words 90 times and contrasting pair of words on 60 occasions.

(v) About 41 per cent poems of *Gitanjali* are songs scattered in different volumes of *Swarabitan.*

(vi) In all 3091 different words used in *Gitanjali* in different frequencies led to 11,521 words altogether[14]. Thus, the number of unique words is more than 1/3 of the total number of words (11521/3091 = 3.73), whereas Zipf considers the number of unique words about 1/10 of the full text. It can be observed from the Table 7.11 that the constant varies widely. Hence, it may be observed that the data do not follow Zipf's law.

It can be observed from a study that the first two words (rank 1 and rank 2) are pronouns, *Amar* (f 205) and *Tomar* (f 199)[15]. The poet offers his prayer to God, so the word Amar (my) and Tomar (your) appears frequently than other words in the whole text. This justifies the title of the *Kavyagrantha* 'Gitanjali' as it is offerings of Tagore to Almighty in the form of songs. It may be noted that Rabindranath wrote in a letter to Indira Devi Chaudhurani ".... *I was not consciously writing poetry when writing the songs of Gitanjali. They were an expression of my feelings; they were my humble prayers, my sincere sadhana and also a reflection of my joys and sorrows*"[16].

Notes and References

1. Tagore, Rabindranath. *Sarodutsav*. Allahabad: Indian Press, 1908.
2. Tagore, Rabindranath. *Gan*. Allahabad: Indian Press, 1908.

3. Mukhopadhyay, Prabhatkumar. *Rabindrajibani O Rabindrasahitya-prabashak*. Vol. 2. Calcutta: Visva-Bharati Granthan Vibhaga, 1994, pp. 227-228.
4. Tagore, Rabindranath. *Gitanjali: Song offerings*. London: The India Society, 1912, p. 80.
5. Tagore, Rabindranath. Letter to Kshitimohan Sen, London, 20 June. Kept in Rabindra Bhavana.
6. Robinson, Andrew. *The Art of Rabindranath Tagore*. Calcutta: Rupa and Co, 1989, p. 33.
7. Kundu, Kalian. *Rabindranath and the British Press (1912-1941)*. London: The Tagore Research Centre, 1990, p. 31.
8. Tagore, Rabindranath. *Gitanjali: Songs offerings*. London: Macmillan Publishing Company, 1913, p. 81.
9. Tagore, Rabindranath. *Gitanjali: Songs offerings*. Santiniketan: Rabindra-Bhavana, 1999, p. 274.
10. Tagore, Rabindranath. *Gitabitan*. Calcutta: Visva-Bharati Granthan Vibhaga, 1380 (B.S.), 1p. 034.
11. Tagore, Rabindranath. *Swarabitan*. 60 Vols. Calcutta: Visva-Bharati Granthan Vibhaga, 1982.
12. *Gitimalya* published in the year 1914 after publication of English *Gitanjali*, but poems were written before and included in *Gitanjali* from manuscript.
13. Tagore, Rabindranath. *Gitanjali: Songs offerings*. Santiniketan: Rabindra-Bhavana, 1999, p. 237.
14. Mallick, B.P., Nara, T and Bhattacharaya, N. *Gitanjali: Linguistic statistical analysis*. Calcutta: Indian Statistical Institute, 1994, pp. 3-97.
15. *Ibid*. p. 123.
16. Tagore, Rabindranath. *Chithipatra*. Vol. 5. Calcutta: Visva-Bharati Granthan Vibhaga, 1400 (B.S.), p. 33.

SECTION-III

Tagore in Print: An Assessment of Quality of Publications

Eight

Tagoreana in the Copyright-Free Phase: An Assessment of Quality of Publications

Introduction

The first book of Rabindranath *Kavi-Kahini* was published in the year 1878 by his friend Prabodh Chandra Ghosh. Regarding this publication Rabindranath wrote, "When I was in Ahmedabad with my brother, my friend astonished me by sending this book"[1]. The second one *Banaphul* was published in the year 1880 by the poet's elder brother Somendranath. Sailesh Chandra Majumdar of Majumdar Library was the first professional publisher who first published *Kavyagrantha* (collected works) of Rabindranath in the year 1903-04. Before that Rabindranath had to publish his works using his own fund with the exception of *Kaḍi o Komal* (published in 1886 by People's Library), *Chithipatra* (published in 1887 by Sarat Kumar Lahiri and Co.), and *Panchabhut* (published in 1897 by Sur Company). Books published from Adi Brahmasamaj Jantra were from his own fund given by his father Debendranath Tagore. Sometimes Rabindranath had to face serious scarcity of funds for publication as well as to meet the expenses of Santiniketan Ashrama. Tagoreana (all the intellectual output of Rabindranath) was even sold in half price from bookshops like Sri Sri Chaitanya Pustakalaya, 9 Cornwallis Street, Kolkata in the year 1897 through press advertisement. Even Rabindranath expressed his willingness to give up copyright of his collected works and publications up to *Kshanika* (1900) for only six thousand rupees to any persons in a letter addressed to Priyanath Sen in 1900[2].

Rabindranath established Visva-Bharati Granthan Vibhaga (VBGB), the Publishing Department of the University, in the year 1923 and published the dance drama *Basanta* in the same year. But regular publication started from the year 1925 with the publication of *Puravi.* Before that the publication right of Tagoreana was given to Chintamani Ghosh, owner of Indian Press/Indian Publishing House of Allahabad. In a letter dated 18th September 1922 Rabindranath wrote, "I have given the right of all my Bengali books to Visva-Bharati in a deed and relieved now"[3]. *Vichitra Prabandha* (Miscellaneous Essays) was published with the declaration, "the copyright of these works rest with Bolpur Brahmacharyashram"[4]. According to Tagore's biographer Prabhat Kumar Chintamoni Kar took the responsibility of publishing the poet's publication with the negotiation of Ramananada Chattopadhaya in 1908. The stock value of 100 books published up to 1923 was Rs. 78,000. Chintamanibabu gave his entire stock to Visva-Bharati at the cost of Rs. 26,000 only…"[5].

Prasanta Chandra Mahalanobis served the Granthan Vibhaga as its first director. Right from the beginning, Mahalanobis started to provide detailed information about a book of Rabindranath published by VBGB under the heading "*Path-parichaya*" and included it either at the beginning or at the end of a book. Later on "*Path-parichaya*" termed as '*Granthaparichaya*" and included at the end of the book. *Granthaparichaya* included detailed information about the first publications, later editions, criticism, changes in manuscripts, and Rabindranath's comment on his own writings. Thus VBGB is the pioneer publisher of Bengali book world with special research-based information. The institute published not only collected works on special themes, but also publications of new editions with collection from different editions of the same book. As a result the institute was able to establish itself as a centre for Tagoreana culture and research[6]. For maintaining spelling and pronouncing standard uniformly for all publications of Tagoreana,

Prasantachandra took special care in consultation with Rabindranath. Suniti Kumar Chattopadhyay and Kalidas Nag also helped him in this respect[7]. Thus VBGB from its very beginning tried to be one of the best publishing houses as well as centre for Rabindra culture with its printing and editorial quality, uniform spelling throughout all the publications as well as house style to fulfill Tagore's vision of Samagra Rabindranath and Bisuddha Rabindranath. According to 2006 catalogue there are 864 (Tagore's writings 334, works on Tagore 174, other titles 356) titles with VBGB.

Visva-Bharati enjoyed copyright of Tagoreana (all the intellectual output of Rabindranath Tagore) according to the then existing law up to December 1991. Later, the Indian Parliament increased the copyright period keeping in mind the Tagore's work and Visva-Bharati, from 50 years to 60 years after the expiry of the author. The main argument was to provide Tagore's complete writings (Samagra Rabindranath), accurately (Bisuddha Rabindranath) to the masses at an affordable cost (Sulabh Rabindranath). The extended period came to an end in 2001 following which private publishers also have been publishing Tagore's works. The present study attempts to look at how far the quality has been maintained by the private publishers.

Objectives of the Study

The study has the following major objectives:

- To find out how far the uniqueness or the quality of Tagore's writings are maintained by publishers of all sorts, particularly in the case of impression, illustrations, compositions, font size, compilation, etc.
- To know what kind of publication should be treated as standard.
- To know whether Tagoreana is being published simultaneously by large private publishing houses as well as small and new publishers in Bengali.

- To assess whether the private publishers maintaining any standard with regard to Tagoreana.
- To know what percentage of Tagoreana is being published by private publishers.
- To ascertain whether Visva-Bharati publications more costly.
- To find out what will be the fate of less popular/ commercially non-viable writings of Tagoreana.

Methodology

For comparative study of the items such as publisher, printer, year of publication, page, size, price, ISBN (International Standard Book Number), copyright, illustrations, introduction, etc., the entire publication of Tagoreana by Visva-Bharati and private publishers has been considered. But to know the quality of the literary text, comparison was made in respect of change or deletion of punctuation marks, use of additional punctuation marks, mistakes in spelling, omission/addition of words/sentence, clubbing of paragraph/lines, etc. in Tagoreana (published by Visva-Bharati) before and after expiry of copyright; and post-copyright publications by private publishers at the first page and at the interval of every ten pages. Last edition of Tagoreana published during Tagore's lifetime is considered as standard publication. Because Rabindranath himself used to correct his own manuscripts even after its first published in journals or books. The evidence of such kind of corrections can be observed from the first edition of many titles of Tagoreana like *Europe-Pravasir Patra, Sesh Raksha, Sahaj path 1, Gitabitan, Chandalika*, etc. preserved in Rabindra Bhavana. Research on such kind of corrections had been conducted based on comparative textual study of different editions of Tagoreana published during Tagore's lifetime. Examples of such studies are *Pathantar Chayan: Rabindranather Upanyas*,[8] (selections from different edition: Rabindranath's fiction) *Sonar Tari: Bishoy Pathantar*[9] (Sonar Tari: Subject: Selection from different editions) etc.

Besides Tagoreana published during Tagore's lifetime the source material also includes collected works of Rabindranath published in 27 volumes by Visva-Bharati. *Books in Print from West Bengal and Book Fair Directory* 2002-2010 was consulted to know the publishers publishing Tagoreana after expiry of copyright[10]. Tagoreana published by different publishers after expiry of copyright also comes under purview of source material for this study. The Catalogue of VBGB (Publishing unit of Visva-Bharat in Kolkata) and also catalogue of twenty-five publishers who published Tagoreana after the expiry of copyright were also considered as source material for this study as it helped to know the total number of publications by individual publishers. Initially 186 titles of 25 publishers were consulted for this study. Out of them four titles namely *Gitanjali, Sanchayita, Gitabitan, Galpaguchchha* have been published by maximum number of publishers (N=9) namely Kamini Prakashalaya(45), Juthika Book Stall(18), Patraj Publication(15), Punascha(11), Ashok Book Agency(10), Sahityam(7), Tuli-Kalam(6), Asia Publishing Company(5), Narayan Pustakalaya(4) were finally considered for this study. Other 16 publishers and their number of publications (within bracket) are: United Publishers (15), Granthasambhar(9), Gitanjali(6), Patra Bharati(6), Nirmal Book Agency (5), Mitra and Ghosh(4), Radha Puatakalaya (3), Reflect Publication (3), Das Sahitya Kutir(3), Bookfront Publication Forum (3), Prakash Bharati (2), Sahitya Bharati (2), Babli Prakashani (1), Baksahitya(1), Rajarshi Prakashan(1), Suranjana Prakashani (1).

Publication of Tagoreana by Private Publishers After the Expiry of Copyright

Table 8.1 gives some idea about total number of publishers publishing Tagoreana after December 2001. It is evident that only a meager percentage of publishers are publishing Tagoreana even nine years after the expiry of copyright. Moreover, names of many publishers like Ranar, Nandita, Saroj, etc. are in the Books in Print but books are not available in the market and many publishers have published only one or two books like *Sahaj Path*. Thus, for this study twenty-five publishers were considered.

Table 8.1: Publishers of Bengali Books (2002-2010)

Sl. No.	*Year*	*No. of publishers publishing Bengali books*	*No. of publishers publishing Tagoreana*	*% of publishers publishing Tagoreana*
1.	2002	688	12	1.74
2.	2003	688	12	1.74
3.	2004	755	32	4.24
4.	2005	755	38	5.03
5.	2006	658	38	5.76
6.	2007	656	37	5.62
7.	2008	653	36	5.51
8.	2009	652	36	5.52
9.	2010	629	49	7.79

**Source*: Books in Print from West Bengal and Fair Directory 2002-2010.

A comparative study of the catalogues of all the twenty-five private publishers with Visva-Bharati publications reveals that only 39 titles are published by private publishers after the expiry of 334 copyrighted titles available with VBGB. After exclusion of English publications, translations into other languages and textbooks of Visva-Bharati, the ratio is found to be 282:39. The number of publications of private publishers excludes selective publications from short stories which are part of *Galpaguchchha* (Collection of short stories) published by VBGB. Actually most of the publishers have published books with the titles of one or two short stories like *Khoka Babur Partyabartan*, *Kabuliwala*, *Postmater*, etc., which are selected from *Galpaguchchha*. Another important feature may be observed that most of the publishers published *Gitanjali*, *Sanchayita*, *Gitabitan* and *Galpaguchchha*. The remaining books are mostly novels, one or two dramas and autobiography of Rabindranath. But books on songs, dramas, essays, religious writings, travel, education, rural development and Rabindra Rachanavali are not yet published by private publishers. Publishers getting their books printed from many printers indicate that most of them have no in-house printing press. Leading publishers of Bengali books like Ananda Publishers, Dey's Publishing, Sahityaloke have not yet started publishing Tagoreana and Mitra and Ghosh published only four books. Relatively new publishers with less number of titles in their credit as observed from their current catalogue like Juthika

Book Stall (05 titles), United Publishers (147 titles), Ashok Book Agency (138 titles), Granthasambhar (53 titles), Gitanjali (79 titles), Asia Publishing Company (107 titles), Radha Pustakalaya (144 titles) etc. started publishing Tagoreana who generally publish children's books, classics and books of authors whose copyright expired like Rabindranath Tagore, Saratchandra Chattopadhyay, Bankim Chandra Chattopadhyay, Sukumar Ray, and Dakshinaranjan Ray.

Private publishers started publishing Tagoreana from January 2002. Table 8.2 gives the number of Tagoreana publications brought out by various private publishers.

Table 8.2: Year of First Publication of Tagoreana by Private Publishers

Publishers	*2002*	*2003*	*2004*	*2005*	*2006*	*2007*	*2008*	*2009*	*2010*	*Total*
1. Kamini	39	6								45
2. Juthika	18						1	2	1	22
3. United	15									15
4. Patraj	15									15
5. Punascha	11									11
6. Ashok	8	2								10
7. Granthasambhar	9									9
8. Sahityam	4	2	1							7
9. Gitanjali	4			1	1					6
10. Tuli-kalam	5			1					1	7
11. Patra Bharati	4	2								6
12. Nirmal	1	4								5
13. Asia	5									5
14. Narayan	4						1			5
15. Mitra and Ghosh		3			1					4
16. Radha					3					3
17. Reflect	3					23	56			82
18. Das Sahitya Kutir	2	1								3
19. Bookfront	3					4	1	1		9
20. Prakash Bhavana										2
21. Sahitya Bharati										2
22. Babli	1									1
23. Bak Sahitya		1								1
24. Rajarshi			1							1
25. Suranjana		1				4	7		1	13

From Table 8.2 it is clear that 81 per cent (151 out of 186) books were published in the year 2002 immediately after the expiry of copyright. Nearly 13 per cent (22 out of 186) books were published in the year 2003 and the remaining 6 per cent books published in the last three years (2004-06). Moreover, most of the books published in 2002 were in between January to May 2002. The year of publication has not been mentioned in case of *Sesher Kavita* published by *Gitanjali* and two titles each of Prakash Bhavana and Sahitya Bharati entitled *Sisu Bholanath* and *Jivansmriti* and *Sahaj path* part-1 and II respectively. Thus, majority of publishers published books in a hurry immediately after the expiry of copyright which increased the possibility of mistakes.

Tagoreana and International Standard Book Number (ISBN)

International Standard Book Number (ISBN) allotted by Raja Rammohun Roy Library Foundation, Kolkata is an important tool for bibliographic control. Tagoreana published by Visva-Bharati incorporated it. So a study of Tagoreana published after the expiry of copyright by private publishers with ISBN may reveal the real situation in this respect.

From Table 8.3 it is clear that five publishers (Patraj, Punascha, Mitra and Ghosh, Reflect and Book Front) published Tagoreana with ISBN. In other words, five publishers out of twenty-five (i.e. 20%) published Tagoreana with ISBN.

Regarding copyright declarations only three publishers (Granthasambhar, Mitra and Ghosh, and Reflect) had clearly mentioned that they reserved the copyright. Five publishers (Kamini, Punascha, Sahityayan, Juthika and United) mentioned the title as the publisher's first edition but without any sign of copyright. The remaining 17 publishers are silent regarding copyright issue.

Comparison of Price of Tagoreana Published by Visva-Bharati and Private Publishers

For marketing of books, besides sales channel, discount structure, advertisement etc. price plays a vital role. It is more important after the expiry of copyright as no monopoly of Visva-Bharati exists now. Table 8.4 will help to have an idea about comparative price of

Table 8.3: Tagoreana Published by Private Publishers with ISBN

Publisher	With ISBN	Without ISBN	Total	Percentage of Titles with ISBN
1. Kamini		45	45	00
2. Juthika		22	22	00
3. United		15	15	00
4. Patraj	15		15	100
5. Punascha	11		11	100
6. Ashok		10	10	00
7. Granthasambhar		9	9	00
8. Sahityam		7	7	00
9. Gitanjali		6	6	00
10. Tuli-kalam		7	7	00
11. Patra Bharati		6	6	00
12. Nirmal		5	5	00
13. Asia		5	5	00
14. Narayan		5	5	00
15. Mitra and Ghosh	4		4	100
16. Radha		3	3	00
17. Reflect	82		82	100
18. Das Sahitya Kutir		3	3	00
19. Book Front	9		9	100
20. Prakash Bhavana		2	2	00
21. Sahitya Bharati		2	2	00
22. Babli		1	1	00
23. Bak Sahitya		1	1	00
24. Rajarshi		1	1	00
25. Suranjana		13	13	00

titles, as discount structure of all the publishers are almost the same i.e. 33.3 per cent to booksellers.

Table 8.4: Comparative Statement of Price: VBGB and Private Publishers (Price is in Rs.)

Title	*VBGB*	*Ka-mini*	*Juthi-ka*	*Patraj*	*Punascha*	*Ashok*	*Sahityam*	*Tuli-Kalam*	*Asia Pub*	*Narayan*
Gitanjali	50	40	30	40	35	25	16	30	60	45
Sanchayita	160	100	100	110	90	130	80	80	125	120
Gitabitan	325	100	120	120	90	150	100	100	150	130
Galpaguchchha	225	110	120	120	110	110	100	80	150	130

It is evident from the above table that the price of all the four titles of VBGB publication is higher than any other private publishers. Except *Gitanjali* three titles namely *Sanchayita, Gitabitan, Galpaguchchha* of Visva-Bharati in the comparative table are hardbound. Books published by private publishers are hardbound (except *Gitanjali published by* Sahityam) but the binding quality is poor. The price of *Gitanjali* — bilingual edition of Asia Publishing seems to be higher but the price of the same edition of Visva-Bharati is much higher i.e. Rs. 125.00.

Comparison of Page and Size of Tagoreana Published by Visva-Bharati and Private Publishers

Price is related to number of pages, size of the book, paper and printing quality, illustrations, etc. So, a comparative statement of pages along with size of the book may throw some light on the above aspect of comparative price statement.

From the Table 8.5 it is clear that the number of pages of the books published by VBGB is much higher in comparison to the number of pages of books published by private publishers (except *Gitanjali* published by Asia which is bi-lingual edition with higher price) though the size remains more or less same. Thus, it is evident that to keep price low, the private publishers compromised on paper, binding and printing quality, font size, space between lines and also top and bottom margins which in many cases violate aesthetic beauty and also publishing quality.

Textual Comparison of Tagoreana Published by Private Publishers and Visva-Bharati

In the first literary comparison (Table 8.6) punctuation marks used in the books published by private publishers and punctuation marks used in Visva-Bharati edition have been compared. Similarly, the second Table (8.6a) shows additional punctuation marks used in the text. In the third Table (8.6b) spelling mistakes, omission or addition of words(s) or line(s), paragraph/line clubbed/separated are considered. Here a line in case of poems considered as a paragraph.

Table 8.5: Comparative Statement of Page and Size: VBGB and Private Publishers

Title	*VBGB*	*Kamini*	*Juthika*	*Patraj*	*Punascha*	*Ashok*	*Sahityan*	*Tuli-Kalam*	*Asia Pub.*	*Narayan*
Gitanjali	194 18×12	152 21.7×13.7	104 22×13.5	128 22×14	176 21.8×14	128 21.7×13.6	151 17.5×12.2	192 21.5×13.5	239 19×10.5	176 21.7×14
Sanchayita	918 21.8×14.5	736 21.7×13.7	606 22×14	607 21.5×14	575 21.8 ×14	664 21.9×13.7	632 22×14.3	780 22×14	640 21.7×14	722 22×13.8
Gitabitan	1034 21.8×14.5	784 21.7×13.7	764 22×14	706 22.3×14	660 21.8×14	784 22.3×14.2	783 22×14.5	959 22×14	824 22×14	764 21.8×14
Galpaguchchha	882 21.5×14.5	848 21.7×13.7	768 22×14	848 22×14	672 21.8×14.5	879 22.1×14.2	896 22×14.5	800 22×14	904 22×14	848 22×13.8

Note: First figure in the 2nd to 10th column represent number of pages and the second, the figure size.

Table 8.6: Textual Comparison: Kamini Prakashalaya, Punctuation Marks: Punctuation Marks Changed or Omitted

Titles	*Page No. Compared*	.	,	:	;	?	!	“ ” ‘ ’	,	—	-	*Total*
Gitanjali	15											0
Sanchayita	70	3	1				1				2	7
Gitabitan	70	4	3						1	1	1	10
Galpaguchchha	84	1	11				4		1		5	22

Table 8.6a: Punctuation Marks: Additional Punctuation Used

Titles	*Page No. Compared*	.	,	;	:	?	!	“ ” ‘ ’	,	—	-	*Total*
Gitanjali	15											0
Sanchayita	70											0
Gitabitan	70											0
Galpaguchchha	84		1									1

Table 8.6b: Other Mistakes

Title	*Page Compared*	*Spelling Mistake*	*Sentence Omitted*	*Word Omitted*	*Sentence Added*	*Word Added*	*Para Clubbed*	*Para Separated*
Gitanjali	15							
Sanchayita	70	1						
Gitabitan	70	3	1	1				
Galpaguchchha	84	3						

During the study it was observed that important access point to enter the thought content like first line index was not used in *Sanchayita* published by Kamini. From the above comparative table it is clear that *Gitanjali* is the best book published by Kamini Prakashalaya with no mistake. On the other hand *Galpaguchha* and *Gitabitan* posses good number of mistakes.

Table 8.7: Textual Comparison: Juthika Book Stall, Punctuation Marks: Punctuation Marks Changed or Omitted

Titles	*Page No. compared*	.	,	:	;	?	!	“ “ ‘ ‘	,	—	-	*Total*
Gitanjali	10		6				1	2	1	6	3	19
Sanchayita	59	1	1						2		2	6
Gitabitan	70		4						1		1	6
Galpaguchchha	77	1	8		1			1	2		1	14

Table 8.7a: Punctuation Marks: Additional Punctuation Marks Used

Titles	*Page No. compared*	.	,	:	;	?	!	" " ' '	'	—	-	*Total*
Gitanjali	10		3						2		4	9
Sanchayita	59											0
Gitabitan	70		2				1					3
Galpaguchchha	77											0

Table 8.7b: Other Mistakes

Title	*Page Compa-red*	*Spelling Mistake*	*Sentence Omitted*	*Word Omitted*	*Sentence Added*	*Word Added*	*Para Clubbed*	*Para Separa-ted*
Gitanjali	10	1						
Sanchayita	59	1		1				
Gitabitan	70	1						
Galpaguchchha	77	5						

In *Gitabitan* published by Visva-Bharati in the index reference of the songs of *Swarabitan* (book of notation) is given, but publication by Juthika lacks it. From the above comparative study it may be concluded that the publisher has not given proper attention in use of punctuation marks even in *Gitanjali*.

Table 8.8: Textual Comparison: Patraj Publications, Punctuation Marks: Punctuation Marks Changed or Omitted

Titles	*Page No. Compared*	.	,	:	;	?	!	" " ' '	'	—	-	*Total*
Gitanjali	12		1									1
Sanchayita	60	1	3					1		1		6
Gitabitan	72	2	1					1		1		5
Galpaguchchha	85	2	18		4		7	3			1	35

Table 8.8a: Punctuation Marks: Additional Punctuation Marks Used

Titles	*Page No. Compared*	.	,	:	;	?	!	" " ' '	'	—	-	Total
Gitanjali	12		1									1
Sanchayita	60		1									1
Gitabitan	72								1		3	4
Galpaguchchha	85		4						3		1	8

Table 8.8b: Other Mistakes

Title	*Page Compa-red*	*Spelling Mistake*	*Sentence Omitted*	*Word Omitted*	*Line Added*	*Word Added*	*Para Clubbed*	*Para Separa-ted*
Gitanjali	12						5	
Sanchayita	60	3						
Gitabitan	72	5		2		5		
Galpaguchchha	85	6				1	3	

A quick look into the Table 8.8 would reveal that the highest and lowest number of other punctuation marks used or not given are *Galpaguchchha* and *Gitabitan*. Similarly, the highest and lowest number of additional punctuation marks used is again in *Galpaguchchha* and *Sanchayita*. One important thing that can be observed is even in case of *Gitanjali* there are mistakes in all the three categories. Clubbing of lines on five occasions in 12 pages obviously affects meter, mora and rhythm of the poems of *Gitanjali*.

Table 8.9: Textual Comparison: Punascha, Punctuation Marks: Punctuations Marks Changed or Omitted

Titles	*Page No. Compared*	.	,	:	;	?	!	“ “ ‘ ‘	'	—	-	*Total*
Gitanjali	17											0
Sanchayita	57	2								1	1	4
Gitabitan	66		1							1	2	4
Galpaguchchha	65	31	117	2	32	3	11	11	1	17	53	278

Table 9a: Punctuation Marks: Additional Punctuation Marks Used

Titles	*Page No. Compared*	.	,	:	;	?	!	“ ” ‘ ’	'	—	-	*Total*
Gitanjali	17											0
Sanchayita	57		1									1
Gitabitan	66		1						1		3	5
Galpaguchchha	65		37						3	1	38	79

Table 9b: Other Mistakes

Title	*Page Compared*	*Spelling Mistake*	*Sentence Omitted*	*Word Omitted*	*Sentence Added*	*Word Added*	*Para Clubbed*	*Para Separated*
Gitanjali	17							
Sanchayita	57	3						
Gitabitan	66			2		3		
Galpaguchchha	65	52				14	7	1

From the comparative Tables (8.9, 8.9a, 8.9b) of books published by Punascha and Visva-Bharati it is clear that special care for publication of *Gitanjali* has been taken as it has no mistake in all the three categories. *Galpaguchchha* published with all kinds of mistakes in all the three categories. *Swaralipipanji* is an important reference of notation to the songs omitted in *Gitabitan* and Rabindranath's dedication of *Ghare-Baire* to Pramathanath Chowdhury not included.

Table 8.10: Textual Comparison: Ashok Book Agency, Punctuation Marks: Punctuation Marks Changed or Omitted

Titles	*Page No. Compared*	.	,	:	;	?	!	" " ' '	'	—	-	*Total*
Gitanjali	12		1									1
Sanchayita	62	2	5		4	2	5	1		3	3	25
Gitabitan	72	1	4				2				2	9
Galpaguchchha	88	2	8		5		2				11	28

Table 8.10a: Punctuation Marks: Additional Punctuation Marks Used

Titles	*Page No. Compared*	.	,	:	;	?	!	" " ' '	'	—	-	*Total*
Gitanjali	12		1									1
Sanchayita	62		2						1			3
Gitabitan	72	1	3							1		5
Galpaguchchha	88	1	8						1		2	12

Table 8.10b: Other Mistakes

Titles	*Page Compared*	*Spelling Mistake*	*Sentence Omitted*	*Word Omitted*	*Line Added*	*Word Added*	*Para Clubbed*	*Para Separated*
Gitanjali	12			1			1	
Sanchayita	62	5						
Gitabitan	72	2	2					
Galpaguchchha	88	10						

The publisher has no book without any mistakes. In Visva-Bharati edition of *Gitabitan*, Saralipipanji, subject and photograph indexes as well as first-line-of-the-song index are provided, but the edition brought out by Ashok Book Agency lacks all these important references.

Table 8.11: Textual Comparison: Sahityam, Punctuation Marks: Punctuation Marks Changed or Omitted

Titles	*Page No. Compared*	.	,	:	;	?	!	“ ” ‘ ’	’	—	-	*Total*
Gitanjali	14											0
Sanchayita	62	1								3		4
Gitabitan	71		5		1		1		1			8
Galpaguchchha	89	12	28	1	4	1	4			5	30	85

Table 8.11a: Punctuation Marks: Additional Punctuation Marks Used

Titles	*Page No. Compared*	.	,	:	;	?	!	“ ” ‘ ’	’	—	-	*Total*
Gitanjali	14											0
Sanchayita	62											0
Gitabitan	71		2									2
Galpaguchchha	89	1	23		1				1		3	29

Table 8.11b: Other Mistakes

Title	*Page Compared*	*Spelling Mistake*	*Sentence Omitted*	*Word Omitted*	*Sentence Added*	*Word Added*	*Para Clubbed*	*Para Separated*
Gitanjali	14							1
Sanchayita	62	1					8	
Gitabitan	71	3						
Galpaguchchha	89	8		1		1		2

Galpaguchchha published by Sahityam possesses the highest number of mistakes relating to the category 'other punctuation marks used, not used or additional marks used (.96,.35 per page respectively). On the other hand, the best production is *Gitanjali* as far as punctuation marks are concerned; only one line of the first poem is divided into two lines. *Galpaguchchha* is having the highest number of spelling mistakes (8 in 89 pages compared) and *Sanchayita* the highest number of paragraphs (line in case of poem) clubbed. However, it does not hamper the flow or rhythm of the poems as all these clubbing are in places and dates of writing at the end of the poem.

Table 8.12: Textual Comparison: Tuli-Kalam, Punctuation Marks: Punctuations Marks Changed or Omitted

Titles	Page No. Compared	.	,	:	;	?	!	" " ' '	,	—	-	Total
Gitanjali	18										1	1
Sanchayita	77	7									1	8
Gitabitan	89	7								1		8
Galpaguchchha	77	31	186		23	7	27	30	11	30	122	467

Table 8.12a: Punctuation Marks: Additional Punctuation Marks Used

Titles	Page No. Compared	.	,	:	;	?	!	" " ' '	,	—	-	Total
Gitanjali	18		1									1
Sanchayita	77											0
Gitabitan	89								1			1
Galpaguchchha	77	1	79		1				6		36	123

Table 8.12b: Other Mistakes

Title	Page Compa-red	Spelling Mistake	Sentence Omitted	Word Omitted	Sentence Added	Word Added	Para Clubbed	Para Separated
Gitanjali	18							
Sanchayita	77				1		2	
Gitabitan	89	1						
Galpaguchchha	77	56					21	2

The mistakes in respect of other punctuation marks used or omitted can be noticed in *Galpaguchchha* (6.07 per page) and additional punctuation marks used in *Galpaguchchha* (1.60 per page). The highest number of spelling mistakes can also be observed again in *Galpaguchchha* (.73 per page). The second line of poem number XXIII of *Gitanjali* (it is bi-lingual edition) in page 155 starts with small letter ('the' used instead of 'The'). In *Gitanjali*, the important reference of *Kavyagrantha* wherefrom the poems are taken is not given.

Table 8.13: Textual Comparison: Asia Publishing Company, Punctuation Marks: Punctuation Marks Changed or Omitted

Titles	*Page No. Compared*	.	,	:	;	?	!	“ ” ‘ ’	’	—	-	*Total*
Gitanjali	21	3	14			1	4	2	9		7	40
Sanchayita	57	2	1				2		24		1	30
Gitabitan	69	2							33			35
Galpaguchchha	73		2						13		1	16

Table 8.13a: Punctuation Marks: Additional Punctuation Marks Used

Titles	*Page No. Compared*	.	,	:	;	?	!	“ ” ‘ ’	’	—	-	Total
Gitanjali	21		8				2				9	19
Sanchayita	57											0
Gitabitan	69											0
Galpaguchchha	73										1	1

Table 8.13b: Other Mistakes

Title	*Page Compared*	*Spelling Mistake*	*Sentence Omitted*	*Word Omitted*	*Line Added*	*Word Added*	*Para Clubbed*	*Para Separated*
Gitanjali	21	8					39	
Sanchayita	57	24						
Gitabitan	69	48						
Galpaguchchha	73	125						

Even in the publication of *Gitanjali* proper care has not been taken as a result it conations 40 mistakes in other punctuation marks used or omitted group, 19 additional punctuation marks have been used and 8 spelling mistakes noticed in 21 pages compared. Not only those in 39 occasions lines are clubbed which certainly hampers the spirit, rhythm, even changes the meaning of poems in *Gitanjali*. In the content part of *Sanchayita* place, date of writing of poems is not provided like Visva-Bharati edition.

Table 8.14: Textual Comparison: Narayan Pustakalaya, Punctuation Marks: Punctuation Marks Changed or Omitted

Titles	Page No. Compared	.	,	:	;	?	!	“ “ ‘ ’	,	—	-	Total
Gitanjali	15											0
Sanchayita	70	3	1				1				2	7
Gitabitan	70	4	3						1	1	1	10
Galpaguchchha	84	1	11				4		1		5	22

Table 8.14a: Punctuation Marks: Additional Punctuation Marks Used

Titles	Page No. Compared	.	,	;	:	?	!	“ ” ‘ ’	,	—	-	Total
Gitanjali	15											0
Sanchayita	70											0
Gitabitan	70											0
Galpaguchchha	84		1									1

Table 8.14b: Other Mistakes

Title	Page Compared	Spelling Mistake	Sentence Omitted	Word Omitted	Line Added	Word Added	Para Clubbed	Para Separated
Gitanjali	15							
Sanchayita	70	1						
Gitabitan	70	3	1	1				
Galpaguccha	84	3						

Gitanjali is the best book published by Narayan Pustakalaya with no mistakes. *Galpaguchchha* contains maximum punctuation mark mistakes (26 per page) and *Gitabitan* contains the highest number of spelling mistakes (3 in 70 pages compared) and sentence and word omitted (1 in each category). As a whole in comparison to other publishers Narayan Pustakalaya gave emphasis in proof reading. It is interesting to note that Narayan Pustakalaya commits the same mistakes as done by Kamini Prakashalaya in *Sanchayita*, *Gitabitan* and *Galpaguchchha*.

Discussion

It was observed during the study that though most of the books published by private publishers are hardbound, the binding as well as paper and printing quality in general is poor. Regarding design of cover page Visva-Bharati follows a house style of saffron cover (with such exceptions as *Raktakarabi*, *Chhinnapatra*, *Natir puja*, *Khapchhada*, *Chandalika* and *Sey*) which is the symbol of sacrifice with title and signature of Rabindranath Tagore in front cover in brown or red and Visva-Bharati logo, price and ISBN at the back cover. Out of 186 titles consulted at the initial stage of this study, cover pages of 64 books contain photograph of Rabindranath, 21 contain paintings and drawings of Rabindranath, and theme of the story is drawn in 89 titles and 12 titles with theme and Rabindranath's photo both. The cover page with theme is mostly scene of cinematography of Rabindranath's popular novels.

In case of Tagoreana published by Visva-Bharati, either there is an introduction by Rabindranath Tagore himself (with the exception in *Gitanjali* where the introduction is by W.B. Yeats) or without any introduction. In most of the cases books published by private publishers included the introduction of Rabindranath whenever available and at the same time introduction written by some others also included. It is interesting to note that Sudeb Mukhopadhyay (no official address given) wrote introductions for three publishers: Kamini Prakashalaya (in 14 books), United Publisher (in 2 books) and Granthasamhar (in 2 books). The same introduction was used thrice in *Gitanjali* published by three publishers. Other persons to introduce Tagoreana are Kamakshiprasad Bandyopadhyay (no address given)—one book entitled *Khapchhada* of Kamini Pustakalaya; Tarun Mukhopadhyay (Department of Bengali, University of Calcutta)—eleven books published by Juthika; renowned literary personality Prof. Prabitra

Sarkar—two books of Punascha; Amitava Basu (home address given) and Basanta Bhattacharyay (no address given)—book of Ashok Book Agency, Dr. Parthajit Gangyopadhyay and Tirthapati Datta—one title each *Galpaguchchha* and *Chhelebela* respectively for Tuli-Kalam; writer Sunil Gangyopadhyay for five titles of Patra Bharati; Dr. Alok Kumar Sen (no address given) for all the four titles *(Gitanjali, Sanchayita, Gitabitan, Galpaguchchha)* of Narayani. As most of the introducers did not give their official or residential addresses questions are likely be raised about the authenticity and also academic credibility to introduce Tagoreana.

In a good number of books published by Visva-Bharati, Granthaparichaya has tremendous research value as it provides information regarding first publication, change in manuscript by Rabindranath, criticism, Rabindranath's own interpretation, etc. Out of 41 titles of Visva-Bharati compared, 23 have this kind of Granthaparichaya. Most of the private publications of Tagoreana lack this kind of Granthaparichaya though publishers like Patraj in *Sanchayita* and *Gitabitan* included Granthaparichaya of Visva-Bharati. It is worthy to note here that this Granthaparichaya section was not written by Rabindranath, in later period it was added with the book by VBGB, first initiated by Charuchandra Bhattacharya. So copying of Granthaparichaya is a clear violation of copyright. Only in ten books (two of Kamini—*Gitanjali* and *Gitabitan;* three of Tuli-Kalam-*Gitabitan*, *Galpaguchchha*, *Lipika*; four of Patrabharati—*Sesher Kavita, Malancha, Chaturanga, Char Adhyay*; one of Nirmal Book agency—*Khapchhada)* Granthaparichaya has been added as publishers own contribution, but a large portion of it is copied from VBGB.

Conclusion

From the above discussion it may be concluded that most of the private publishers published Tagoreana with low price which resulted in poor quality in respect of physical as well as intellectual part of the thought content with huge number of punctuation-mark mistakes, spelling mistakes, line/word omission/addition, and paragraph clubbed/separated. Mistakes in any kind of punctuation mark either addition, omission or exchange affects the meaning, meter, mora and rhythm of writings. This is especially true in case of literature. Change of words, sentences, mistakes in spelling are obviously an indication of injustice to the author. Specially when, regarding corrections of manuscripts, its publications in journals or book Tagore was very careful[11].

Only a small portion of private publishers (5.78%) are publishing Tagoreana in Bengali and the leading publishers are yet to start publishing Tagoreana. The interest of private publishers was high immediately after expiry of copyright as maximum number (81%) of titles was published in 2002. A very small portion of commercially viable and fast saleable titles of Tagoreana (13.83%) has been published by private publishers even five years after the expiry of copyright. Thus, though Tagoreana is now available easily at less cost but '*Bisuddha Rabindranath*' as well as '*Samagra Rabindranath*' are still distant dreams. Thus publishers publishing Tagoreana in the copyright free world should be more careful and that would be the best way to pay homage in the 150th birth anniversary to the greatest literary personality, India had ever produced.

References

1. Tagore, Rabindranath. *Jibansmriti*. Calcutta: Visva-Bharati Granthan Vibhaga, 1405 (B.S.), p. 161.
2. *Visva-Bharati Granthan vibhaga: Panchasatvarsha Parikrama: 1923-73*, Calcutta: Visva-Bharati Granthan Vibhaga, 1974, pp. 12-14.
3. Das, Anathnath. *Visva-Bharati Granthanvibhaga*; in Basu, A.K. Ed. *Saraswat: A collection of profiles of some learned bodies of West Bengal.* Kolkata: Paschim Bangla Bangla Academy, 2008, p. 317.
4. Tagore, Rabindranath. *Vichitra Prabandha*. Calcutta: Visva-Bharati Granthan Vibhaga, 1907, p. 149.
5. Mukhopadhyaya, Prabhatkumar. *Rabindrajibini o Rabindrasahitya-prabasha*, Vol. 3. Calcutta: Visva-Bharati Granthan Vibhaga, 1961, p. 145.
6. *Visva-Bharati Granthan Vibhaga o Charuchandra Bhattacharyya.* Calcutta: Visva-Bharati Granthan Vibhaga, 1984, p. 54.

7. Das, Anathnath. *Visva-Bharati Granthanvibhaga.* in Basu, A.K. Ed. *Saraswat: A collection of profiles of some learned bodies of West Benga.* Kolkata: Paschim Bangla Bangla Academy, 2008, p. 317.
8. Bhattacharyay, Amitrasudan. *Pathantar chayan: Rabindra upanyas.* Calcutta: Visva-Bharati Granthan Vibhaga, 1410 (B.S.), p. 272.
9. Ghosh, Debkumar. *Sonar tari: Bishay pathantar.* Hooghly: Sahityao Desh, 1987, p. 174.
10. *Books in print from West Bengal and fair directory: 2002-2006.* Kolkata: Publishers and Booksellers Guild.
11. Bagchi, Sanat Kumar. *Rabindranather pandulipi: Samiksha o bisleshasa.* Kolkata: Punthi Pustak, 1989, p. 335.

Nine

100 Years of Publication of Gitanjali: A Study

Introduction

Rabindranath composed his first poem at the age of eight and by the end of his life at the age of eighty, he has written twenty-five volumes of poetry, fifteen plays, ninety-five short stories, eleven novels, thirteen volumes of essays; initiated and edited various journals; prepared Bengali textbooks, penned thousands of letters; and crossing the age of seventy created more than two thousand paintings. It starts with the publication of the first poem signed in his own name *Hindu Melar Upahar* (The Gift of Hindu Mela) and first verse narrative *Banaphul* (The Wild Flower) was published in *Gnanankur* and *Pratibimbo*. The last birth day of Rabindranath (7th May 1941) is marked with the publication of three books, one in verse *Janmadine* (On my Birthday), one comprising short stories, *Galpasalpa* and the English version of *Chhelebela* (Boyhood days).

Rabindranath Tagore's long literary career has been classified by different scholars from different viewpoint of his literary development. Chunkapura classified it as youth and early adulthood writings (1878-1900), *Gitanjali* period (1900-1912), the years of matured reflections (1912-1927) and the final years (1927-1941)[1]. Thompson classitied development of Tagoreana as early life and poetry (1861-1886), The *Shileida* and *Sadhana* period (1887-1897), unrest and change (1898-1905), *Gitanjali* period (1905-1919) and finally internationalism (1919-1941)[2]. Majumder[3], Prabhatkumar[4], Kripalani[5] divided the literary life of the poet in different epochs. Regarding this Tagore rightly observed "...It is discerned in the analysis of those who look at it and study it from outside. But the author is unaware of it. To the author the moments of creation, the seasons of flowering and fruit-gathering are what matters; that is what touches him emotionally"[6]. It is obvious that the growth of Tagoreana (all the intellectual output of Rabindranath Tagore) with the passage of time reflected faithfully the diverse tendencies of his age.

Whatever may the classification, there is no doubt that translation of his 'spiritual' poems in English "*Gitanjali*" in 1912 and Nobel Prize for literature on 13th November 1913 for it has a special impact globally. The recommendation within Swedish Academy came from another winner of the Nobel Prize — Werner von Heidenstam. He wrote that he had read no lyric writing to equal Tagore's in the previous twenty years or more. "They gave me hours of intense enjoyment; it was like drinking the water of a fresh, clear spring... There is nothing in his work that is controversial and offensive, nothing vain, worldly and petty, and if ever a poet may be said to possess the qualities that make him entitled to the Nobel Prize, it is he"[7]. *The Daily Mail* (Nov. 14, 1913; p. 7, Col 13) under the heading Nobel Prize for an Indian Poet quotes W.B. Yeats "I know of no man in my life time who has done anything in the English language equal to Mr. Tagore's lyrics"[8]. It has again rightly been reflected in citation of Oxford DLitt *honoris causa* on Tagore in 1940 "Here before you is the myriad-minded poet and writer" ('poeta et scriptor myrianous')[9]. That was an appropriate description of the vast range of Tagore's literary creations in the form of poetry, drama, songs, essays, novels and short stories.

Objectives of the Study

The study has the following major objectives:

- To trace the origin and growth pattern of the poems of *Gitanjali* scattered in different *Kavyagrantha* (books of poems);
- To understand the publishing scenario of Tagoreana in general and *Gitanjali* in particular before and after the expiry of copyright in 2001; and
- To assess the quality of publication of *Gitanjali* before establishment of VBGV and also post copyright publication by private publishers' with that of Visva-Bharati.

Source and Methodology

For assessing publication of *Gitanjali* before establishment of VBGV its first publication by India Society of London on 1st November 1912 and subsequent publication by Macmillan and Company in March 1913, London compared with manuscript and original Bengali poems scattered in different *Kavyagrantha.*

For post copyright textual comparison of *Gitanjali,* its bilingual edition published by Tagore research centre Rabindra-Bhavana was consulted as the source document as Bengali poems of this edition has been taken from the last publication (1941) of *Gitanjali* published during Tagore's life time and as it is bilingual, so a comparative study is possible[10]. Last edition of Tagoreana published during Tagore's lifetime is considered as standard publication. Because Rabindranath Tagore, himself used to correct his manuscripts. The evidence of such kind of corrections can be observed from the first edition of many titles of Tagoreana like *Europe-Pravasir Patra, Sesh Raksha, Sahaj Path 1, Gitabitan, Chandalika* etc., preserved in Rabindra Bhavana, Santiniketan. Research on such kind of corrections had been conducted based on comparative textual study of different editions of Tagoreana published during Tagore's lifetime. Examples of such studies are *Pathantar Chayan: Rabindranather Upanya*[11]] (selections from different edition: Rabindranath Tagore's fiction) *Sonar Tari: Bishoy Pathantar*[12] (*Sonar Tari*: Subject: Selection from different editions) etc. The editions of India Society and Macmillan were also consulted to assess pre Visva-Bharati publication of *Gitanjali.*

Books in Print from West Bengal and Book Fair Directory 2002-2010 was consulted to know the publishers publishing Tagoreana after expiry of copyright[13]. Tagoreana published by different publishers after expiry of copyright also comes under purview of source material for this study. The catalogue of Visva-Bharati Granthan Vibhaga and also catalogue of twenty-five publishers who published Tagoreana after the expiry of copyright were also considered as source material for this study as it helped to know the total number of publications by individual publishers.

One hundred and ninety-five titles of twenty-six publishers were consulted for this study. Out of them, four titles namely *Gitanjali, Sanchayita, Gitabitan, Galpaguchchha* have been published by maximum number of nine publishers namely, Kamini Prakashalaya (45), Juthika Book Stall (18), Patraj Publication (15), Punascha (11), Ashok Book Agency (10), Sahityam (7), Tuli-Kalam (6), Asia Publishing Company (5) and Narayan Pustakalaya (4), Parul (9). The other 16 publishers publishing Tagoreana and their number of publications (within bracket) are: United Publishers (15), Granthasambhar (9), Gitanjali (6), Patra Bharati (6), Nirmal Book Agency (5), Mitra and Ghosh (4), Radha Puatakalaya (3), Reflect Publication (3), Das Sahitya Kutir (3), Bookfront Publication Forum (3), Prakash Bharati (2), Sahitya Bharati (2), Babli Prakashani (1), Baksahitya(1), Rajarshi Prakashan(1) and Suranjana Prakashani (1).

To evaluate the quality of the literary text, comparison was made in respect of change or deletion of punctuation marks, use of additional punctuation marks, mistakes in spelling, omission/addition of words/sentence, clubbing of paragraph/lines, etc. in *Gitanjali* published by Visva-Bharati and post-copyright publications by private publishers at the first page and at the interval of every ten pages.

Pre Visva-Bharati Publication

Gitanjali in Bengali was published in September 1910 with 157 songs and poems. Out of these songs 20 were previously published by Indian Press, Allahabad, in *Shārodutsav*[14] in 1908 and *Gān*[15] in

1909. The remaining 137 poems and songs were written in 90 days in between August 1909 to August 1910 (10th Bhadra 1316 to 29th Shravan 1317 (B.S.)[16]. Rabindranath Tagore himself took the task of the translation of *Gitanjali (Song Offerings)* when he sailed for England on 27th May 1912. There he handed over the poems to William Rothenstein whom he met earlier in Calcutta in the year 1911. Moved by the poems Rothenstein in turn gave the poems to W.B. Yeats to read. The literary and artistic circle of Yeats decided to publish the poems after Yeats made a selection of them and wished to write an introduction to it. That is how *Gitanjali* was first published by India Society of London on 1st November 1912. It was written in the half title page of the publication that "seven hundred and fifty copies of this edition have been printed for the India Society of which two hundred and fifty copies only are for sale"[17]. Regarding this Rabindranath wrote to Kshitimohan Sen "... I feel he must be happy with my writing and wants others to share that happiness. It is something like our taking delight in the lotus we offer him because he delights in it. I feel he has brought me from East to West..."[18].

The next edition of *Gitanjali* was published in the next year (March 1913) by Macmillan and Company, London. The number of poems in Bengali and English *Gitanjali* are not the same. In Bengali there were 157 poems, but in English it was 103. The poems were first published in different *Kavyagrantha*. At the end of the Indian edition of India Society or Macmillan there was a statement: "These translations are of poems contained in three books—*Naivedya, Kheya* and *Gitanjali*—to be had at the Indian Publishing House, 22 Cornwallis Street, Calcutta; and of a few poems which have appeared in periodicals"[19]. But this information is not complete as the poems were collected from ten other 'books of poems' (Table 9.1).

In fact, even a comparative study of *Gitanjali* published by India Society, London and Macmillan edition besides punctuations, change can be noticed such as in poem number 52 one can observe in Indian Society edition

.no more coyness and sweetness of demeanor. *(Page 47)*

Table 9.1: Poems of *Gitanjali* from Different *Kavyagrantha*

Sl. No.	Book	Year of publication	No. of poems
1.	*Chaitali*	1912	1
2.	*Kalpana*	1900	1
3.	*Naivedya*	1901	15
4.	*Smaran*	1903	1
5.	*Shishu*	1903	3
6.	*Utsarga*	1903	1
7.	*Kheya*	1906	11
8.	*Gitanjali*	1910	53
9.	*Achalayatan*	1912	1
10.	*Giti-malya*[20] *(collected from the manuscript for Gitanjali, before publication as book in 1914)*	1914	16
	Total		**103**

But the same line in Macmillan edition has changed as:

> …no more shy and soft demeanour.

These changes have been made comparing them with the manuscript and according to Yeats' suggestions. Even there were some mistakes in the first line of the content of India Society publication (the poem number and correct line is given in the bracket) such:

> Prisoner, tell me, who it was (31)
> (Prisoner, tell me, who was it);
>
> Let only that little remain of me (34);
> (Let only that little be left of me);
>
> Hast thou not heard his silent steps? (45);
> (Have you not heard his silent steps?);
>
> When first they came out, the warriors (85);
> (When the warriors came out first);
>
> When I give up the helm, then the time has come (99);
> (When I give up the helm, I know that the time has come).

Even by scientific comparison of original Bengali poems and English translation one can find,

(i) In the English translation number 61 of *Khoka* from *Shishu* the last two stanzas were deleted.
(ii) In the second line of translation number 71 "amar" has been translated as "thy" but actually it is "tomar".
(iii) The translated poem number 95 comprises two poems; complete poem number 89 of *Naivedya* and last stanza of 90th poem in Bengali,
(iv) Only the first part of the poem "*Utsarga*" has been translated in the English translation number 102.

Visava-Bharati Publication

In the year 1923, Rabindranath Tagore established Visva-Bharati Granthan Vibhaga (VBGV), the Publishing Department of the University with the publication of his dance drama *Basanta.* Before that the publication right of Tagoreana was given to Chintamani Ghosh, owner of Indian Press/Indian Publishing House of Allahabad. In his letter dated 18th September 1922 Rabindranath Tagore wrote, "I have given the right of all my Bengali books to Visva-Bharati in a deed and relieved now"[21]. *Vichitra Prabandha* (Miscellaneous Essays) was published with the declaration, "the copyright of these works rest with Bolpur Brahmacharyashram"[22]. According to Tagore's biographer Prabhat Kumar Mukhopadhyaya "Chintamoni Kar took the responsibility of publishing the poet's publication in 1908. The stock value of 100 books published up to 1923 was Rs. 78,000. Chintamanibabu gave his entire stock to Visva-Bharati at the cost of Rs. 26,000 only..."[23].

Prasanta Chandra Mahalanobis as the first director of VBGV introduced "*Path-parichaya*" later on renamed as *Granthaparichaya* on Tagoreana providing details information about the book and included it at the beginning or end of the books. *Granthaparichaya* provided details information about a particular book in respect of its first publication, later editions, criticism, changes or corrections in manuscripts, and Rabindranath Tagore's comment on his own writings. For maintaining spelling and pronouncing standard uniformly for all publications of Tagoreana, Prasanta Chandra took special care in consultation with Rabindranath Tagore. Suniti

Kumar Chattopadhyay and Kalidas Nag also helped him in this respect[24]. Thus VBGV established as one of the best publishing houses as well as centre for Rabindra culture with its printing and editorial quality, uniform spelling throughout all the publications as well as house.

Bengali *Gitanjali* containing 157 poems (161 pages) first published in Bhadra, 1317 (1910) by VBGV. In the introduction Rabindranath admits that some songs given in the beginning of this book published in other books. Up to Jaistha, 1413 (2007), 40th reprint of this edition of *Gitanjali* published. In the first line index of the poems reference of the notations of the songs in *Swarabitan* (book of notations) is also given. 42 poems of *Gitanjali* are songs (Rabindra Sangit), source of notations of different volumes of *Swarabitan* of these songs are given in content. After publication of *Gitanjali* English edition, reference of English translations also provided at the end. Rabindra Bhavana, Tagorean research and cultural centre published bilingual edition of *Gitanjali* in December 1999 which provides W.B. Yeats introduction at the beginning, *Granthaparichaya* and alphabetical first line index of both Bengali and English poems provided at the end. Another bilingual edition of Gitanjali with facsimile reproduction of Bengali manuscripts only published by VBGV in collaboration with UBS Publishers' Distributors in 2003 after expiry of Tagore's copyright. This edition is made on map litho glossy paper with 304 pages, in the size 24.5 X 18.5 cm. and price Rs. 495. On the background of English poems murals and pictures of Santiniketan, provided. At the end along with Yeats introduction, Nobel prize acceptance speech, introduction of some other renounced translations of *Gitanjali* into foreign languages such as Andre' Gide's introduction to his French translation, Storniolo's prologue of Portuguese translation of *Gitanjali* provided. But no index is provided.

Publication of Gitanjali After Expiry of Copyright

The extended period of copyright of intellectual output of Rabindranath Tagore given to Visva-Bharati expired in December 2001. Private publishers have been free to publish the writings of

Rabindranath Tagore since then. But from Table 9.2, it can be seen that a small number of publishers are publishing Tagoreana after December 2001. Names of many publishers like Ranar, Nandita, Saroj, etc. are given in the Books in Print but books are not available in the market. Several publishers have published only one or two books like *Sahaj Path*.

Table 9.2: Publishers of Bengali Books (2002-2010)

Sl. No.	*Years*	*No. of publishers publishing Bengali books*	*No. of publishers publishing Tagoreana*	*Percentage*
1.	2002	688	12	1.74
2.	2003	688	12	1.74
3.	2004	755	32	4.24
4.	2005	755	38	5.03
5.	2006	658	38	5.76
6.	2007	656	37	5.62
7.	2008	653	36	5.51
8.	2009	652	36	5.52
9.	2010	629	49	7.79

**Source*: Books in Print from West Bengal and Fair Directory 2002-2010.

A comparative study of the catalogues of all the twenty-six private publishers with Visva-Bharati publications reveals that only 39 titles are published by private publishers after the expiry of 334 copyrighted titles available with VBGV. After exclusion of English language publications, translations into other languages and textbooks of Visva-Bharati, the ratio is found to be 282:39. The number of publications of private publishers excludes selective publications from short stories which are part of *Galpaguchchha* (Collection of short stories) published by VBGV. Most of the publishers have published books with the titles of one or two short stories like *Khoka Babur Partyabartan, Kabuliwala, Postmater*, etc., which are selected from *Galpaguchchha*. Another feature observed was that most of the publishers published *Gitanjali, Sanchayita, Gitabitan* and *Galpaguchchha*. The remaining books are mostly novels, one or two dramas and autobiography of Rabindranath Tagore. But books on songs, dramas, essays, religious writings, travel, education, rural development are not yet published by private publishers. Publishers getting their books printed from many printers indicate that most of them have no in-house printing press. It is observed from a study that 81 per cent (151 out of 186) books were published in the year 2002 immediately after the expiry of copyright. Nearly 13 per cent (22 out of 186) books were published in the year 2003 and the remaining 6 per cent books were published in the last three years (2004-06). Moreover, most of the books published in 2002 were in between January to May 2002[25].

Comparison of Price of Gitanjali Published by Visva-Bharati and Private Publishers

Table 9.3 shows that the price of *Gitanjali* published by VBGV is higher than private publishers. Books published by private publishers are hardbound (except *Gitanjali published by* Sahityam) but the binding quality is poor. The price of *Gitanjali* — bilingual edition of Asia Publishing seems to be higher but the price of the same edition of Visva-Bharati is much higher i.e., Rs. 125.

Table 9.3: Comparative Statement of Price: Visva-Bharati Granthan Vibhaga and Private Publishers

(In Rs.)

Title	*VBGB*	*Kamini*	*Juthika*	*Patraj*	*Punascha*	*Ashok*	*Sahityam*	*Tuli-Kalam*	*Asia Pub*	*Narayan*	*Parul*
Gitanjali	100 125 (bilingual edition)	40	30	40	35	25	16	30	60	45	75 (HB) 60 (PB)

Comparison of Page and Size of Gitanjali by Visva-Bharati and Private Publishers

Price is related to number of pages, size of the book, paper and printing quality, illustrations, etc. So, a comparative statement of pages along with size of the book may throw some light on the above aspect of comparative price statement.

Table 9.4 shows that the number of pages of the books published by VBGV is higher as compared to the number of pages of books published by private publishers (except *Gitanjali* published by Asia which is bi-lingual edition with higher price) though the size remains more or less the same. To keep price low, the private publishers have compromised on paper, binding and print quality. Further, it was observed that the font size, space between lines and also top and bottom margins in many cases have compromised aesthetics.

Textual Comparison of Gitanjali Published by Visva-Bharati and Private Publishers

In the first literary comparison (Table 9.5), punctuation marks used in the books published by private publishers and punctuation marks used in Visva-Bharati edition have been compared. Similarly, the second Table (9.5a) shows additional punctuation marks used in the text. In the third Table (9.5b) spelling mistakes, omission or addition of words(s) or line(s), paragraph/line clubbed/separated are considered. For poems, a line is considered as a paragraph.

Mistakes in publication of Gitanjali in different categories can be observed from the above Tables (9.5, 9.5a, 9.5b). Clubbing of lines on five occasions in 12 pages by Patraj or in 39 occasions in 21 pages compared by Asia Publishing House obviously affects spirit, rhythm, even changes the meaning of poems in *Gitanjali*. Change of punctuation marks in 40 times (21 pages compared) and 41times (26 pages compared) by Asia Publishing House and Parul is really injustice to a poet like Rabindranath. It is also evident that care has been taken for publication of *Gitanjali* by some publishers like Punascha, Narayan as it has no mistakes.

Discussion

Most of the books published by the private publishers are hardbound but the binding as well as paper and printing quality in general is poor. Regarding design of cover page, Visva-Bharati books have a saffron cover (with such exceptions as *Raktakarabi, Chhinnapatra, Natir puja, Khapchhada, Chandalika* and *Sey*), with signature of

Table 9.4: Comparative Statement of Page and Size (In Cm): Visva-Bharati Granthan Vibhaga and Private Publishers

Title	VBGB	Kamini	Juthika	Patraj	Punascha	Ashok	Sahityan	Tuli-Kalam	Asia Pub.	Narayan	Parul
Gitanjali	194 18×12	152 21.7×13.7	104 22×13.5	128 22×14	176 21.8×14	128 21.7×13.6	151 17.5×12.2	192 21.5×13.5	239 19×10.5	176 21.7×14	303 17.5×111.5 311. 17.5×12

Note: First figure in each row against the book title represents number of pages and the second figure in each row represent dimension in centimeters.

Table 9.5: Punctuation Marks Changed or Omitted

Publishers	*Page no. compared*	.	,	:	;	?	!	“ ” ‘ ’	’	__	-	*Total*
Kamini Prakashalaya	15											0
Juthika Book Stall	10		6				1	2	1	6	3	19
Patraj Publications	12		1									1
Punascha	17											0
Ashok Book Agency	12		1									1
Sahityam	14											0
Tulu-Kalam	18										1	1
Asia Publishing Company	21	3	14			1	4	2	9		7	40
Narayan Pustakalaya	15											0
Parul (HB Ed.)	26	2	9		2	2	4	10		12		41
Parul (PB Ed)	25	2	11			2			5	19		39

Table 9.5a: Additional Punctuation Marks Used

Publishers	*Page no. compared*	.	,	;	:	?	!	“ ” ‘ ’	’	__	-	*Total*
Kamini Prakashalaya	15											0
Juthika Book Stall	10		3						2		4	9
Patraj Publications	12		1									1
Punascha	17											0
Ashok Book Agency	12		1									1
Sahityam	14											0
Tuli-Kalam	18		1									1
Asia Publishing Company	21		8				2				9	19
Narayan Pustakalaya	15											0
Parul (HB Ed)	26		4	1						5		10
Parul (PB Ed)	25	6		1			1		7	6		21

Table 9.5b: Other Mistakes

Publishers	*Page no. compared*	*Spelling mistake*	*Sentence omitted*	*Word omitted*	*Sentence added*	*Word added*	*Para clubbed*	*Para separated*
Kamini Prakashalaya	15							
Juthika Book Stall	10	1						
Patraj Publications	12						5	
Punascha	17							
Ashok Book Agency	12			1			1	
Sahityam	14							1
Tuli-Kalam	18							
Asia Publishing Company	21	8					39	
Narayan Pustakalaya	15							
Parul	26	8					4	
Parul (PB Ed)	25	6					3	12

Rabindranath Tagore on the front cover in brown or red and Visva-Bharati logo, price and ISBN at the back cover. But title cover page of *Gitanjali* published by private publishers had photograph of Rabindranath Tagore and/or replica of his paintings and drawings.

Bilingual edition of *Gitanjali* published by Visva-Bharati provides *Granthaparichaya* which has tremendous research value as it provides information regarding first publication, change in manuscript by Rabindranath Tagore etc. and first line index of both English and Bengali poems. W.B. Yeats introduction to *Gitaanjali* also provided. Bengali *Gitanjali* along with *Granthaparichaya,* first line index of songs with the name of *Kavyagrantha* and volume of *Sarabitan* (book of notation) also provided. But private publishers did not include this kind of information. Only *Gitanjali* published by Kamini *Granthaparichaya* has been added as publishers own contribution, but a large portion of it is copied from Visva-Bharati Granthan Vibhaga. Bilingual hardbound edition of Parul published in 2010 translated Yeats English introduction into Bengali and index of first line index of both English and Bengali songs provided at the end. But the first line is not complete as a result sometimes it becomes meaningless. In paperback edition instead of Yeats introduction in *Gitanjali,* Tagore's Nobel Prize acceptance speech in English and its Bengali translation provided.

Conclusion

Regarding corrections of manuscripts, its publications in journals or book Rabindranath was very careful[26]. Mistakes in one kind or other can be observed since the publication of *Gitanjali* in 1912. But post copyright publications of Tagoreana by private publisher, besides poor quality paper, binding and printing contain a lot of mistakes. Mistakes in other titles of Tagoreans published by private publishers are much higher than Gitanjali[27]. Mistakes in any kind of punctuation mark either addition, omission or exchange affects the meaning, meter, mora and rhythm of writings. This is especially true in case of literature. Change of words, sentences, mistakes in spelling are obviously an indication of injustice to the authors. Publishers publishing Tagoreana in general and *Gitanjali* in particular should be very careful especially in the eve of 100th year (1912-2012) of publication of *Gitanjali*.

Notes and References

1. Chunkapura, Jose. *The God of Rabindranath Tagore: A study of the evolution of his understanding of God*. Calcutta: Visva-Bharati Granthan Vibhaga, 2002, p. 351.
2. Thompson, Edward. *Rabindranath Tagore: Poet and dramatis*. Calcutta: Rddhi-India, 1979, p. 335.
3. Majumdar, Bimanbehari. *Heroines of Tagore: A study in the transformation of Indian society 1875-1941*. Calcutta: Firma K.L. Mukhopadhyay, 1968, p. 15.
4. Mukhopadhyaya, Prabhatkumar. *Life of Tagore*. New Delhi: Indian Book Company, 1975, p. 208. Tr. from Bengali by Sisirkumar Ghosh.
5. Kripalani, Krishna. *Rabindranath Tagore: A Biography*. Calcutta: Visva-Bharati Granthan Vibhaga, 1980, p. 491.
6. Tagore, Rabindranath. *Introduction to Collected Works, Vol. 1*. Calcutta: Visva-Bharati Granthan Vibhaga, 1939, pp. 9-11.
7. Robinson, Andrew. *The Art of Rabindranath Tagore*. Calcutta: Rupa & Co, 1969, p. 33.
8. Kundu, Kalian. *Rabindranath and the British Press (1912-1941)*. London: The Tagore Research Centre, 1990, p. 31.
9. Bhattacharya, Sabyasachi. *Rabindranath Tagore: An Interpretation*. New Delhi: Viking, 2011, p. 5.
10. Tagore, Rabindranath. *Gitanjali: Songs offerings*. Santiniketan: Rabindra-Bhavana, 1999, p. 274.
11. Bhattacharyay, Amitrasudan. *Pathantar chayan: Rabindra upanyas*. Calcutta: Visva-Bharati Granthan Vibhaga, 2002, p. 272.
12. Ghosh, Debkumar. *Sonar tari: Bishay pathantar*. Hooghly: Sahitya O Desh, 1987, p. 174.
13. *Books in print from West Bengal and fair directory: 2002-2010*. Kolkata: Publishers and Booksellers Guild.
14. Tagore, Rabindranath. *Sarodutsav*. Allahabad: Indian Press, 1908.
15. Tagore, Rabindranath. *Gan*. Allahabd: Indian Press, 1908.
16. Mukhopadhyay, Prabhatkumar. *Rabindrajibani O Rabindrasahitya-prabashak*. Vol. 2. Calcutta: Visva-Bharati Granthan Vibhaga, 1994, pp. 227-228.

17. Tagore, Rabindranath. *Gitanjali: Song offerings*. London: The India Society, 1912, p. 80.
18. Tagore, Rabindranath. *Letter to Kshitimohan Sen*. London, 20 June. Kept in Rabindra Bhavana.
19. Tagore, Rabindranath. *Gitanjali: Songs offerings*. London: Macmillan Publishing Company, 1913, p. 81.
20. *Gitimalya* published in the year 1914 after publication of English *Gitanjali*, but poems were written before and included in *Gitanjali* from manuscript.
21. Das, Anathnath. *Visva-Bharati Granthanvibhaga*; in Basu, A.K. Ed. *Saraswat: A collection of profiles of some learned bodies of West Bengal*. Kolkata: Paschim Bangla Bangla Academy, 2008, p. 317.
22. Tagore, Rabindranath. *Vichitra Prabandha*. Calcutta: Visva-Bharati Granthan Vibhaga, 1907, p. 149.
23. Mukhopadhyaya, Prabhatkumar. *Rabindrajibini o Rabindrasahitya-prabasha*, Vol. 3. Calcutta: Visva-Bharati Granthan Vibhaga, 1961, p. 145.
24. Das, Anathnath. *Visva-Bharati Granthanvibhaga*; in Basu, A.K. Ed. *Saraswat: a collection of profiles of some learned bodies of West Bengal*. Kolkata: Paschim Bangla Bangla Academy, 2008, p. 317.
25. Ray, P. P., Quality assessment of copyright free Tagoreana: A study, *Annals of Library and Information Studies*. 58 (5) (2011) 257-269.
26. Bagchi, Sanat Kumar. *Rabindranather pandulipi: samiksha o bislehasan*. Kolkata: Punthi Pustak, 1989, p. 335.
27. Ray, P. P. *Tagore in print: A comparative study before and after expiry of copyright*. New Delhi: Concept Publishing, 2012, p. 199.

Index